D1492571

CHARLOTTE
CORDAY

PORTRAIT OF CHARLOTTE CORDAY
From a painting by J. J. Hauer at Versailles

CHARLOTTE CORDAY

By
MICHEL CORDAY

Translated from the French by
E. F. BUCKLEY

THORNTON BUTTERWORTH, LTD.
5, BEDFORD STREET, LONDON, W.C.2.

First published – – – 1931

PREFACE

DURING my childhood, my paternal grand-father, whose surname was Pollet, often used to tell me that we were related to Charlotte Corday and therefore to Corneille, and reminded me that his own mother, whose maiden name was Morand de la Genevraye, was a cousin of Charlotte Corday.

So when I had to adopt a pseudonym for writing, I turned to this family tradition. I was still in the Army when I published my first books and at that time an officer was not allowed to write under his own name. But I may add that, at the express wish of my children, I took the necessary legal steps to change my name to Michel Corday.

It is this tradition that spurred me on to write a life of Charlotte Corday, for I wanted to leave my four grandchildren, Pierre and Lise, Yvette and Claude, a history of their " cousin ". I must also mention that I had occasion just recently to write two biographical essays, and I thought I might as well complete the trilogy. I was the friend of Anatole France during the last twelve years of his life, and after his death I felt I must perpetuate in book form the most important things I knew about him and had heard from his own lips. Shortly afterwards, I was asked to contribute to a series an account of the romantic life of some great person‹age, and I chose Diderot, for whom I have the profoundest love and admiration.

But, in the present case, the task I have under‹taken is peculiarly delicate. I soon saw that it would force me to reach a more considered and definite opinion on various important subjects, such as revolutionary violence, the influence of Corneille, and the right to kill. I also had to refer to all the authorities I had consulted in writing my physio‹logical novels, in order to examine by the feeble light of science the phenomenon of a young girl of gentle birth, of sweet and virtuous disposition and well‹balanced mind, who had never left her native province, allowing herself to be overcome, subju‹gated and driven straight to her goal by the unswerv‹ing determination to go to Paris for the purpose of killing the Friend of the People.

For nearly a year I prepared for the task I had undertaken. I made pilgrimages to Charlotte Cor‹day's native district; I visited museums; I haunted libraries; I hunted for books that had been lost, and discovered treasures that few had set eyes upon.

The glass cases I have pored over! The people I have questioned!—custodians of museums and librarians, some expansive and eager, others shy and retiring; stern keepers of archives, busy journalists, venerable bibliophiles and aged booksellers curiously detached from the Age and from life itself.

I have sometimes been inclined to think that a description of my exciting and varied researches would provide far more lively and interesting reading than the book for which I was collecting material.

Everywhere I was met only with goodwill and an eager readiness to help. In case I forget anybody, I shall mention no names. But each one of my temporary colleagues will know what share to take of the thanks I address to all.

CONTENTS

LIST OF ILLUSTRATIONS

pardonnés moi mon Cher papa d'avoir disposé de mon existence
sans votre permission, j'ai vengé bien d'innocentes victimes, j'ai —
prévenu bien d'autres désastres, le peuple un jour désabusé, se
réjouira d'être délivré d'un tyran, si j'ai Cherché a vous persuadé
que je passais en angleterre Cesque j'esperais garder l'incognito mais
jen ai Reconnu l'impossibilité, j'espere que vous ne serés point tourmenté
en tous Cas je Crois que vous aurés des defenseurs a Caen, j'ai pris
pour defenseur gustave Doulcet, un tel attentat ne permet nulle
defense C'est pour la forme, adieu mon Cher papa je vous —
prie de m'oublier ou plutôt de vous Réjouir de mon sort la
Cause en est Belle, j'embrasse ma soeur que j'aime de tout
mon Coeur ainsi que tous mes parens, n'oubliés pas Ce vers de
Corneille
Le Crime fait la honte Et non pas l'Echafaud

C'est demain a huit heures que l'on me juge, Ce 16 juillet

Corday

FACSIMILE OF LETTER WRITTEN BY CHARLOTTE CORDAY
WHILST IN PRISON THE DAY BEFORE HER TRIAL.

CHARLOTTE CORDAY

CHAPTER I

THE ABBAYE⸱AUX⸱DAMES

IN THE summer of 1789, a year which was to
prove epoch⸱making in her life, Charlotte
Corday had just reached the age of twenty⸱one.[1]
The flower of her youth had just unfolded, and
no better moment could be chosen to draw her
portrait. The picture of her can be conjured up
in a few words—she was a woman of Normandy.
Tall, with ample bosom, a dazzling complexion,
and pronounced though refined features, she was,
as it were, the symbol of the land which for eight
hundred years had been the cradle of her ancestors.[2]
Her whole country was reflected in her. Her
cheeks had the fresh bloom of apple⸱blossom in
which milky whiteness gradually merges into the
pink of the rose. Veiled beneath long lashes and
heavy lids, her gentle intelligent eyes changed from

grey to blue like the sea round the Normandy coast. Her hair, the colour of ripe corn, also varied according to the light from fair to brown, and her curly, almost frizzy locks, clustered about the classic oval of her face and dove-white neck, falling down over her shoulders. She had heavy, arched eye-brows, a drooping though firmly moulded nose, a fresh, full mouth, and a prominent chin curiously divided in two by a vertical cleft like a peach.

At this period, she was still a boarder at the Abbaye de la Sainte Trinité, which was also called the Abbaye-aux-Dames, at Caen. She did not wear the habit of the nuns of the community, the black dress relieved by white veil and headband. But although her blue uniform was almost monastic in its simplicity, it revealed the natural beauty of her figure. She had an air of sweet, grave modesty, a proud bearing, a harmonious gait, and hands with beautiful tapering fingers.

Her low, sweet voice, with its clear refined accents, was in keeping with her personality, and its extraordinarily musical calibre and almost childlike purity made it a delight to the ear.

In spite of every effort on the part of those about her to cure her of the defect, she was fond of hanging her head in an attitude of dreamy melancholy.

.   .   .   .   .

Melancholy? How could she have failed to fall
beneath the burden of melancholy in the shadow
of the heavy arches of the Abbaye-aux-Dames? As
far as her memory served her, that is to say from
about the age of five, her life had been divided into
two distinct halves. First came a childhood spent
in the open air, in cornfields and orchards, in woods
and sunlight, a childhood full of the fragrance of
cider and new-mown grass, a childhood of light linen
dresses leaving her neck and arms bare. Then
suddenly everything grew dark and over-clouded;
she was put into a tight, high-necked uniform and
shut up between the forbidding walls of the Abbey.

During the free and easy days of her early girl-
hood she had frequently changed her abode. But
all the houses in which her childhood was passed
are grouped together,[3] and form a little constella-
tion on the map, clustering between Argentan and
Vimoutiers, at the entrance to the Vallée d'Auge,
that broad stretch of pasture-land stretching down
to the sea, on which the fat backs of the cattle, put
out to grass, stand out like glossy rocks.

Le Ronceray, where she was born in 1768, in
Saint-Saturnin-des-Ligneries, and a similar house in
the neighbourhood, now known as the Ferme des
Bois, both belonged to her father, Monsieur de
Corday d'Armont. They were typical Normandy

farmhouses, of brick and wood, one story high, standing in the middle of an orchard. The place that Charlotte loved best was the Château de Mesnil-Imbert, a house of proportions almost as modest as the two just mentioned, the home of her paternal grandfather, Corday de Cauvigny. But she also had her own room at the Château de Glatigny, a more imposing structure, with its curved beams and fine panelling, which belonged to her uncle, Corday de Glatigny.

She left these four houses, which were all in the same neighbourhood, only on an occasional visit to another of her uncles, the Abbé de Corday, the curé of Vicques. It was in the presbytery of Vicques that she learnt to read from a volume of Corneille soiled with age and use, which had been reverently preserved by the Abbé. And he constantly reminded her that she was the great-grand-daughter of the famous tragic poet,[4] and taught her to admire him at the same time as she learnt to read his works. All the Cordays were extremely proud of their illustrious ancestor.

The whole family extended their hospitality to the little girl. They were anxious to help her parents and to ease their burdens, for Monsieur de Corday was not at all well-off. He had three daughters and two sons, and his wife was delicate.

The right of primogeniture, of which he was a victim, had left him only an extremely small property which he cultivated himself with more zeal than practical knowledge.

Poverty was all the more irksome to him since he was extremely charitably disposed. He used to seize every opportunity for helping anybody who was worse off than himself, and sought out hidden cases of distress from house to house in the village. A touching tribute was long current in the district: "The Cordays," it was said, "were poor, but the poor never knew it."

For Charlotte her wandering childhood was an extremely happy period of her existence. She spent the greater part of her time at the Château de Mesnil✦Imbert, with her grandparents, and was a great favourite with the old couple and their daughter, Mademoiselle de Cauvigny; while their servant, Fanchon Marjot, nicknamed Marjote, adored her and was her devoted slave. When she was an old woman, she held the name of Charlotte Corday in such reverence that she took up her abode in a tiny room which had been the favourite retreat of her heroine as a child.

This room was above the bakehouse and the little girl used to spend whole afternoons there reading. Reading was a passion with her. In this room she

B

used to collect the village children and teach them to read, sew and sing, and after she went to the convent as a boarder she kept up the habit when she came home for the holidays. As it was a lace-making district, she taught them the *Point de France*, and gave them all sorts of dainties to eat. She had inherited her father's love of helping and making presents.

It was at this time that two characteristics of her nature became more plainly marked—she was devoted to others and quite regardless of her own interests. Her indifference to herself amounted almost to physical insensitiveness. One day, when she was about twelve years old, she had a bad fall, but though she was pale and bleeding, she smilingly assured her people that she was all right, and refused to confess that she was in pain. " Ah ! " cried her mother, " the child is so hard on herself. She never complains ! I have to guess when she is ill. She would never tell me."

Life at Mesnil-Imbert was not so lively and gay as it was at Glatigny, where, in her uncle's house, Charlotte had the companionship of a band of rowdy young cousins of both sexes. But, as a matter of fact, there was constant intercourse between the two houses, which were quite close to each other. In the winter, as soon as there was a fall of snow,

the first duty of the inmates was to clear the great
elm grove which joined the two estates, so that
communications should not be interrupted. And
whatever the season, the children used to sound a
lively summons from one house to the other on the
horn.

This band of young people threw themselves
heart and soul into the little social amusements of
the district, which Charlotte took a lead in organiz-
ing. Generally serious and grave, she had sudden
outbursts of gaiety, just as she also had fits of shy-
ness. Thus she would remain silent throughout a
meal, but as soon as she had left the table, she would
join most eagerly in all the simple games and
amusements.

If dumb things could speak, the panelling of
Glatigny could tell of many a mad game of blind-
man's buff in which, should the blind man happen
to catch his cousin Charlotte, he never failed to
recognize her by her crisp, curly hair which seemed
almost alive in his hands.

.   .   .   .   .

Suddenly everything changed.

In 1782, Monsieur de Corday d'Armont went to
Caen to follow a lawsuit in which he was engaged
against his wife's brothers, the Gautiers. He took

his family with him and lived in lodgings in the Butte St. Gilles. Here, shortly afterwards, Charlotte lost her elder sister and then her mother, the latter dying in giving birth to a sixth child, who did not survive.

Monsieur de Corday was devoted to his wife, and, although they were still young, their friends used to call them Philemon and Baucis. He was pros/ trate with grief. He stayed on as a widower in his temporary lodgings with his four children and lived in a state bordering on penury. Charlotte and her younger sister Éléonore, it is true, kept house as best they could. Their father used to leave what little money he possessed in an open drawer, and this sign of confidence made them do their utmost to be economical. But their elder brother was destined for the Army, and his education was expensive !

It was at this juncture that Madame de Belzunce came upon the scene. She had for many years been head of the Abbaye/aux/Dames, which was in the close vicinity of the Cordays' lodgings in the Butte St. Gilles. She soon learnt of the father's straitened circumstances and the devotion of the daughters, and took an interest in the two sisters, touched by the beauty of the one and the misfortune of the other; for Éléonore was a hunchback.

Theoretically, the Abbaye did not take boarders. The King alone had the right to nominate one or two. But Madame de Belzunce had offered a home to her niece, Alexandrine de Forbin d'Oppède, and suggested to Monsieur de Corday that his two daughters should come to the Abbaye and share in Mademoiselle de Forbin's education. He accepted, and leaving Caen, returned home, while Charlotte and her sister went to the Abbaye⊹aux⊹Dames, where they were destined to remain for nearly ten years.

.   .   .   .   .

On the hill overlooking the capital of Normandy, the Abbaye⊹aux⊹Dames spreads like a little fortress, surrounded by a rampart with turrets at regular intervals. This wall encloses the house of the Abbess, the nuns' quarters, built round a cloister, pleasure gardens, orchards, a flower garden, and a park intersected by elm groves. At the entrance stands a simple grey old church, the body of which is Norman and the spire Gothic.

One of Charlotte's aunts, Madame de Louvagny, was a nun at the Abbey. Her family declared that she had taken the veil because she had been crossed in love; she had been enamoured of a young man and had been forced to marry a grey⊹beard. But time had healed her wound.

Madame de Louvagny was specially charged with the religious education of her nieces, but in the case of Charlotte she met with considerable difficulty at first. On reaching years of discretion, the girl regarded it as her duty to examine the dogmas of the Church. The idea was not new to her, for her uncle, the Abbé de Corday, had already had occasion to complain of her attitude when he was teaching her the rudiments of religion at the presbytery of Vicques. "She disputed everything inch by inch," he used to declare, "and never gave in."

She behaved in the same way now, and in the heat of discussion a little vertical line would appear between her eyebrows, a sort of replica of the little cleft in her chin.

As a matter of fact, she was seeking her own soul. More often than not, she armed herself with the weapons of logic and reason. But on occasion she plunged once again into the waters of faith. At such times she would seek refuge in the crypt under the church to bury herself in the darkest, most silent and lonely retreat, to hold communion with God in prayer and contemplation. She would come back, however, to the daylight and the sun, and with the obstinate little line in her forehead grown deeper, renew her theological discussions with Madame de Louvagny.

Then gradually the silent influence of monotonous practices repeated again and again, and the secret and soothing force of habit, gained the upper hand, and the storm in her breast died down beneath the pressure of regular life and daily routine.

Thenceforward her life flowed smoothly on. She learnt drawing and music,[5] and still read a great deal, especially ancient history. Towards evening she would often take a stroll in the gardens of the Abbess, and from a hillock look down on the roofs from which rose the smoke of the hearth≀fires and the hum of life, and on a wide panorama of pointed belfrys, some massive as fortresses, others of a light aerial beauty. Moreover, she was not cut off from this town that lay so close at her feet. She heard all that went on there. For the Abbess still loved the world, and her pupils helped her to entertain. Charlotte also accompanied the nuns on their visits to the poor. And her longing to devote her life to others was still so strong that in the St. Gilles quarter people long afterwards remembered the young girl whose zeal was even greater than that of her religious companions who had to practise charity by profession.

When she was nearly twenty, the Abbess handed over some of the household duties to her, and she used to do all the correspondence with shop≀keepers and tradespeople.[6] The work was by no means distasteful to her and enabled her to be of some use to the community that sheltered her. She carried out her duties with the practical common-sense of the true native of Normandy, which she had managed to preserve in spite of all the fluctuations and contrasts of her excitable nature. Thus, when the troublous days of the *assignats* came she cleverly safeguarded the interests of the Abbey by laying in a stock of the lace she knew so well and using it as a means of barter.

So, with the practice of a few accomplishments, with reading, walks in the gardens of the Abbess, and charitable or social visits for its only incidents, her simple life passed by like Corpus Christi Day, hung with white and adorned with homely flowers.

.   .   .   .   .

She had been leading this humdrum existence for seven years, when the first rumblings of the Revolution began to be heard. They did not stop short at the gates of the Abbey. On the contrary, they rolled in sonorous echoes beneath its arches, as through a cathedral in which the slightest sound is exaggerated a thousandfold.

The States General! The Bastille! Charlotte hailed the stirring news which seemed to her big with hope. For everything conduced to make her welcome it with enthusiastic fervour.

She had learnt not only to read Corneille, but also to think like Corneille. Her ancestor had left her the legacy of a fierce and fanatical love of liberty.

Moreover, Monsieur de Corday was a member of that Liberal aristocracy whom the ideas of the Encyclopædists and Philosophers had won over to their side. The injustice of the right of primogeni* ture, which he had denounced in a pamphlet, had brought home to him all the abuses of the old system. Last but not least, both father and daughter were imbued with the same compassionate spirit, the capacity of feeling the sufferings of others and the desire to relieve them.

One day there arrived at the Abbey a young man who described all the successes of the Revolu* tion as so many victories. He was Gustave Doulcet de Pontécoulant, the nephew of the new Abbess, Madame de Pontécoulant. Madame de Belzunce, whose colleague she had been, had died on the 31st of January, 1787.[7] Gustave Doulcet, who was twenty*five, was a whole*hearted supporter of the new ideas, and it was chiefly in the presence of Charlotte that he belauded their triumphant pro* gress. Moreover, he was a distant relative of the young boarder; above all, she was the only inmate of the convent who shared his views.

From the very beginning of the Revolution, he had made heavy sacrifices for the faith that was in him, being probably the first man in France to renounce his titles. When the three Estates of the Realm had sent their representatives to the States General, instead of attending the gatherings of the nobility to which he was summoned, he went to the meetings of the bailiwicks at which the Third Estate nominated its representatives. And he had helped to draw up the *cahiers* embodying the demands which the Third Estate in Normandy, as in all the other French provinces, were addressing to the States General. It was an admirable work, for it was in these *cahiers* of the Third Estate that the best of the Revolution came to light. Their aims, wise, broad-minded, clear-sighted and comprehensive though they were, have not been realised even yet, and at the end of a hundred and forty years they still remain *par excellence* the Charter of popular rights.

From a distance Gustave Doulcet was eagerly following the solemn debates that were taking place at Versailles. In June, the deputies of the Third Estate had sworn not to part before giving France a Constitution. The States General had become

the National Assembly, which was afterwards known
as the National Constituent Assembly. Its aim was
to abolish monarchy and substitute the rule of Law,
and, breaking down all resistance on the part of
the Court and the nobility, it cleared a path for
itself through the forest of prejudice. Whilst La
Fayette and Sièyes were drawing up the Declaration
of the Rights of Man,[8] the necessary prelude to the
Constitution, the Paris mob was breaking open the
Bastille.

These successes inspired the nephew of the Abbess
with even greater enthusiasm, and his excitement
knew no bounds when, on the morning of the 7th
of August, a letter reached Caen from Gabriel de
Cussy, one of the deputies for Normandy. During
the night of the 4th–5th of August the National
Assembly had abolished feudal rights and seigniorial
privileges. In an irresistible outburst of generosity
and a frenzied desire to outdo their rivals, in which
the nobility took the lead, it had confirmed the
rights of the citizens and proclaimed that taxes
should be general.

This letter was read in public at the Hôtel de
Ville in Caen, where windows and doors were all
thrown open. The crowd went mad with delight.
The people fell on each other's necks and wept
tears of joy. Deputies from Paris brought further

details. Inequality, hounded down right and left, was a thing of the past! And on the following day a Te Deum, a review and illuminations celebrated this unparalleled event.

Charlotte shared Gustave Doulcet's enthusiasm, though she was well aware that on that night the nobility had been animated as much by considera-tions of prudence as of justice. Almost everywhere the peasants were ransacking the châteaux for papers and old feudal title-deeds, and burning the depositories of records. Sometimes they went even further. In the vestibule of the Château d'Harcourt, the seat of the Governor of Normandy, had they not torn down a heavy statue of Louis XIV? The privi-leged classes were afraid of another peasants' revolt.

But Charlotte, outwardly now grave now gay, was sweetly ironical—another marked characteristic. She had the capacity for seeing the comic element which is always latent in life's tragedies. Clearly all these representatives of the nobility were mere men—fear had driven them to espouse the cause of justice. But this made their action all the more pathetic; it was so essentially human. If at first they had responded only to the call of private interest, they had gradually risen above them-selves, and in a sort of wave of contagious intoxica-tion, had been raised aloft to the sublime.

In six short hours a system established from time immemorial had been destroyed. A social revolution such as the world had never before seen had been carried out amid tears of joy. And not a single drop of blood had been spilt! For Charlotte this wonderful night brought the realisation of her purest dreams. On the next day the sun was to rise on the Golden Age!

.   .   .   .   .

Three days later a terrible scene disgraced the town of Caen.

Vicomte Henri de Belzunce was second in command of the Bourbon regiment. He was said to be the nephew of Madame de Belzunce, but as a matter of fact he was only a distant relative. Moreover, when he went into garrison at Caen in April, 1789, the Abbess had already been dead for two years. He was a young man of twenty*four, slim and good*looking, pale, dark, elegant and haughty. And his passionate devotion to the army and the King was equalled only by his contempt for the people and the Revolution.

In and out of season he gave expression to his feelings with such brilliance, sarcasm and foolhardy arrogance, that his superiors were contemplating his removal. He used to ride through the town followed by soldiers on horse-back, and on the smallest provocation would whip out his pistol.

At the end of June, he aroused the hostility of the mob. On the 29th of that month, Caen heard the news that the Nobility and Clergy had consented to join the Third Estate in the National Assembly, and in joyful celebration of the event a wooden pyramid, painted to resemble blue marble, had been set up in the Faubourg de Vauxcelles. On its three facets it bore the words: " *VIVE LE ROI ! VIVE NECKER ! VIVE LES TROIS ORDRES !* " It was decorated with flowers and wreaths, and in the evening it was illuminated. These rejoicings were extremely distasteful to young Henri de Belzunce, and he molested a little boy who was letting off fireworks, and aimed his pistol at one of the citizens who took the child's part. The murmurs of the crowd died down only when a mounted patrol, which he immediately summoned, formed a cordon round the pyramid.

On another occasion, when he supplied escorts for the corn convoys leaving Caen, he was accused of starving the town, and the rumour was also cir-culated that he wanted to burn it down and shoot the inhabitants. Probably his soldiers had warned the street-women in the neighbourhood of the barracks that he would have no hesitation in firing on the crowd. His haughty bearing and insolent jokes at the expense of the National Government and the civil Guard, added fuel to the fire of sus≠picion.

At last, on the 11th of August, the decisive struggle took place. Henri de Belzunce had incited some of his soldiers to tear off Necker's medal, which was worn by their comrades in the Artois regiment. He even brutally assaulted some of the latter who resisted. They were furious, and made their griev≠ances known in the streets. At about eleven o'clock in the evening, shots exchanged between a civilian sentinel and an army officer succeeded in raising the alarm. The tocsin was sounded, and the rumour ran through the town that the Bourbon regiment had taken up arms against the citizens.

Was this true? The municipality invited Mon≠sieur de Belzunce to offer an explanation. He con≠sented to do so, and left the barracks where he was quartered. But as the crowd pressed round him shaking their fists, the leading men of the place suggested that, for his own safety, it would be better for him to spend the night in the Château, that is to say, the fortress.

On the morning of the 12th, he was taken out and conducted to the Hôtel de Ville. The tocsin, which had begun to ring again as soon as it was light, had attracted a crowd who gathered together even from the outlying districts, and assembled armed with muskets, pitchforks and scythes. Henri de Belzunce, who had been taken by surprise on the previous evening by the alarm, was still in his white dressing-gown and green slippers. He timidly advanced through the maddened mob which was howling for his death.

He knew that he was doomed. During the night in the Château he had already written a farewell letter to his comrades and told them his last wishes. In order to escape terrible torture, he decided to kill himself, and tried to snatch a pistol from one of his guards, who, misunderstanding his action, knocked him down with the butt end of his musket. Amid indescribable confusion, wild firing put an end to him.

The mob hurled themselves on his body and tore it to bits, cutting open his chest with scissors and grabbing the heart. A young plasterer, with red hair and sallow cheeks, his arms covered with blood to the elbows, threw the warm ball up into the air; a woman caught it and sticking the still palpitating flesh on a red-hot spike, ate it.

Others cut off the head and the hands, tore out the entrails and hoisting them on pitchforks marched round the town with them to the beat of drums.

The procession halted at a hairdresser's in Vauxcelles to have the hair on the head curled. Farther
on when it had been spat upon and subjected to
unmentionable indignities, the rabid mob insisted
on passersby, who were too well dressed, kissing it.
Lastly, in the belief that Madame de Belzunce was
still alive, they took the hideous remains, with songs
and shouts and the beating of drums, to the windows
of the AbbayeauxDames.

.   .   .   .   .

Thus within the space of three days both the
bright and the sordid sides of the Revolution had
been revealed to Charlotte Corday.

She had seen men rise above themselves and in a
frenzy of generosity reach sublime heights; vying
with the gods, they had attempted to build the
world afresh. She had also seen the beast let loose
by a contrary passion, satisfying its worst instincts
in blood, cowardly, envious, obscene and a hundred
times more cruel than the most ferocious denizen
of the jungle.

The Revolution after having risen to the heights
had sunk to the depths ! Charlotte was distressed
beyond measure, and her suffering explains her life
and the deed she did.

c

CHAPTER II

CHARLOTTE and her sister left the Abbaye-aux-Dames in April, 1791. Although the monastic orders had been suppressed for almost a year, the nuns were still allowed to live in their convent. But they no longer felt safe. In Caen, by way of a threat, birch rods were sometimes hung on the door of their church. They were the weapon of the mob, and in several places the crowd had flogged women who attended Mass celebrated by refractory priests.

The two young girls returned to their father at the Ferme des Bois. Their elder brother had emigrated and the younger was thinking of joining him. But the Revolution had made life more diffi-cult than ever at home, and Charlotte was quick to perceive it. Unwilling to be a burden on her father, she made up her mind to leave a situation which was equally painful to them both.

At one time she thought of taking the veil, and even chose the institution—the Convent of the

Sœurs de Sainte Claire at Argentan. But Mon‑
sieur de Corday, convinced that his daughter was
sacrificing herself for the sole object of lightening
his burdens, resolutely opposed the idea.

Charlotte gave way; but it was not long before
she became involved in constant political discus‑
sions with her father. She had, as a matter of fact,
outstripped him. The influence of the philosophers
and the injustice of which he himself was the victim,
had opened the eyes of Monsieur de Corday to the
abuses of the established system. But he was very
far from feeling the same enthusiasm as his daughter
for the progress of the Revolution.

Charlotte was following the movement with pas‑
sionate interest. Since the terrible death of Henri
de Belzunce, her faith had not been shaken by
coming into contact with any other atrocity. For
nearly two years no further bloodshed had stained
the records of the Revolution. The Constituent
Assembly was peacefully carrying out its colossal
task of reconstruction, and the mob had escorted
the royal family back from Versailles to Paris in
joyful procession. In an apotheosis, moving in its
grand simplicity, all the provinces had joined in
setting the seal on the national unity on the Champs
de Mars at the great Fête de la Fédération held on the
14th of July, 1790.

Charlotte, anxious to help her father and spare him expense as well as constant irritating disputes, was also eager to follow these great events at closer quarters. She therefore decided to return to Caen and seek shelter with her aunt, Madame de Bretteville. Leaving her sister Éléonore with her father, she bade farewell to her home in June, 1791.

.   .   .   .   .

Madame de Bretteville, as a matter of fact, was not Charlotte's aunt, but her cousin, both being great-grand-daughters of Corneille, a relationship of which they were equally proud. This common bond of sympathy would have been quite sufficient to bring them together, so great was the pride felt by the whole family in their illustrious ancestor.

But on the death of her only daughter in 1788 Madame de Bretteville became more than ever attached to her young relative. Two years later, she lost her father and her husband in quick succession, and this twofold bereavement increased her loneliness and her need for affection.

During the holidays, Charlotte used to spend part of her time at Verson, near Caen, where Madame de Bretteville had a proprety. On the day she left the Abbaye-aux-Dames, her elderly relative herself drove to the convent to fetch her, and when three months later Charlotte begged her hospitality, she welcomed her as though she were her own daughter.

On the death of her father, an eccentric old man who had hoarded up every penny until his dying day, Madame de Bretteville had inherited what was for the time quite a considerable fortune. And when, a few months later, her husband, who was Government Treasurer to the *Bureau des Finances* in Caen, also departed this life, she remained sole mistress of a very substantial property.

She was sixty-seven when Charlotte sought her hospitality. She was a tiny little woman, bent with age and pitted by small-pox. Religious, hide-bound by tradition, and always with a tall white cap on her head, she was reckoned somewhat simple-minded. But her simplicity was not lacking in subtlety, for she was essentially kind and good, and a heart of gold lent her understanding.

The following incident is typical. At the end of 1791 one of her friends, a certain Madame Levaillant, made up her mind to leave Caen, where there had been fresh disturbances, and go to Rouen which was said to be more peaceful. She urged Madame de Bretteville to follow her example. But that good lady, who had remained calm and smiling through the storm, was determined not to desert her home.

Yet she felt it would be invidious to set her friend an example in courage. So she pretended that she was filled with strange and unaccountable fears; nothing on earth, she declared, would induce her to cross the bridge of boats across the Seine at Rouen; it might at any moment be carried out to sea !

Her goodness, though it put an edge to her tongue, also made her charmingly indulgent towards the frailties of others. When she became a widow, she continued to show hospitality to an illegitimate son of Monsieur de Bretteville, whom he had brought home after one of his journeys to distant parts.

Her house, number 148 Rue St. Jean,[9] opposite the Rue des Carmes, was built of solid stone in the Gothic style. In the front of the building, the ground floor, above which there were two stories with three windows, was used as a workshop by a carpenter named Lunel. On the right a low arched doorway opened into a passage from which Madame de Bretteville's private staircase led; it ended in a long narrow paved courtyard with a wall on the right and the house built round the three other sides. In a recess stood a pump.

The room occupied by Charlotte Corday was on the first floor at the bottom of the courtyard. It could be reached direct by a little winding stone staircase with a balustrade, and communicated with Madame de Bretteville's rooms by a long corridor inside the house. It was a huge room lighted by two mullioned windows with little leaded lights. The fireplace, with its projecting mantelpiece, rose from the brick floor to the bare rafters of the ceiling.

On the death of her husband, Madame de Bretteville had turned his room into a drawing-room, placing her own mahogany bureau in it and a marble-topped chest with ormolu embellishments. The curtains were of hand-printed cotton with the design in self-colour. The furniture and easy chairs were upholstered in silk, and hunting pictures hung above the doors and the mirror over the mantelpiece. Here and there were tapestry screens and good engravings—*Abraham repudiating Hagar, Peace, The Conflagration*.

Charlotte and her aunt loved to sit in this room, the windows of which looked out on the Rue St. Jean, and in it they entertained a good many people. The Treasurer's widow had a large circle of friends, the most intimate of whom were Madame Levaillant, Madame Achard, Monsieur Delarue, an official on the municipality, Monsieur Lévêque, President of the Departmental Directorate, and Monsieur Duvi-

vier de Jumilly, the constitutional curé of the parish
of St. Jean.

Madame de Bretteville was a frequent visitor at
the Hôtel de Faudoas which was almost next door.
The Comte de Faudoas was in command of the
National Guard. Here the two women used to meet
members of the oldest families in the town and,
in spite of differences of opinion between them,
Charlotte soon made friends with Éléonore de
Faudoas, who was sixteen at the time.

Yet she (Charlotte) was by no means worldly and
above all cared nothing for dress. Her clothes,
though not devoid of taste, had no style about them.
In the street she would allow her skirts to sweep the
ground. But when she was dressed for a function
she was suddenly transformed, carrying herself with
proud grace and queenly dignity.

She had fits of coquetry, just as she had fits of
gaiety. On her arrival, her aunt supplemented her
slender wardrobe with a quantity of pretty dresses
and as soon as she put one of them on she was a
different person. She even gave up her bad habit
of hanging her head, and her aunt's old friends
had no need to scold her and tell her to show her
eyes and not hide them. " They are far too
beautiful ! " they declared.

.   .   .   .   .

Charlotte's main object in leaving home had been to follow the course of events, and she immediately looked out for people who could supply her with information. These she had no difficulty in finding among her relatives and friends; but the most diligent and enthusiastic of them all she discovered close at hand and almost under the same roof as herself.

At the age of sixty-six, Madame de Bretteville, who had lived for so long under the guidance of her father and her husband, suddenly found herself in possession of a large fortune, and feeling that she could not cope with the responsibility, she very wisely engaged a steward and man of trust.

His name was Augustin Leclerc.[10] He was just twenty-five when Charlotte met him at her aunt's house. The son of a local surveyor, he possessed a little property of his own. He did not actually live in the house in the Rue St. Jean, but used to go there every day. Short and lively, with a round face and snub nose, he breathed intelligence. As discreet as he was clever, he was here, there and everywhere. He managed Madame de Bretteville's affairs, looking after her investments and estates; he kept her house in repair and the two old servants up to their duties.

He was a self-educated man and had attended courses on law, medicine and astronomy. Brought up on the Encyclopædists and the Philosophers, all of whose works he possessed, he had hailed the dawn of the Revolution with the greatest enthusiasm.

In complete agreement with Charlotte on this point, he had immediately entered into an alliance with her. They even had little secrets between them. As he held the purse-strings, he was entrusted with the duty of handing over a certain sum to her once a month for her good works. But Charlotte's charit- able zeal increased with the resources at her com- mand, and she never made her money last to the end of the month. So Augustin Leclerc, though he gently took her to task, would consent to make her an advance unknown to the mistress of the house.

Their main topic of conversation was the Revolu- tion, its progress, and the promise it held forth. They rivalled each other in fiery ardour and mutual exaltation. Leclerc lent Charlotte the works of his beloved philosophers, which were a revelation to her. At the Abbaye-aux-Dames, she had read and re-read Greek and Roman history, Plutarch's " Lives of Illustrious Men " and the tragedies of her great ancestor Corneille. But she now discovered Voltaire and Jean-Jacques Rousseau ! It was like a ray of sunlight amid the ruins.

Augustin Leclerc also recommended her the Abbé Raynal's works, for which he had a particular admiration. He was the last of the Encyclopædists. The rest were all dead and he was the sole survivor. He had been the friend of Diderot who was said to have revised his most famous work, " L'Histoire Philosophique des Deux Indes."

.   .   .   .   .   .

But Charlotte had other sources of information. In the first place, on her return to Caen, she met Gustave Doulcet again. True to his convictions, he had quickly forged ahead, and since the previous year, when the Constituent Assembly had divided France into Departments, he had been head of the administration in Calvados.

But she more often met another young man of the same age as Gustave Doulcet, who was also a whole-hearted convert to the new ideas—Hippolyte Bougon-Longrais. Cultured, witty, energetic, ambit- ious and conscious of his own worth, he was General Secretary of Calvados.[11] Of medium height, he had blue eyes, an aquiline nose and refined manners, and dissimulated his youth beneath a grave de- meanour. His chief asset was his eloquence; he was extremely fluent and spoke in warm sonorous tones.

He used to lend Charlotte newspapers and innumerable pamphlets employed by the various parties to circulate their views and combat their opponents, and they used to discuss, and write to each other about, all manner of historical, political and literary subjects. Charlotte found the relation, ship extremely pleasant and he found it even more so. If she had wanted a husband, she would cer, tainly have chosen Bougon,Longrais.

But she did not want to marry. She had already refused several offers, including one from Monsieur de Boisjugan de Mingré. She had even discouraged the attentions of Monsieur de Tournélis, although the match would have pleased Madame de Brette, ville, to whom the gentleman was distantly related. But on the question of marriage, as on many others, Charlotte was adamant. " You will never put Madame on my letters," she used to assure her friends. " I shall never give up my beloved liberty; never shall any man be my master ! "

Her love of independence only partially explains her abhorrence of the idea of marriage. For she was always under the spell of a vague, inexplicable sense of shame. The whole mysterious subject of love terrified her. Bashful of her own outstanding beauty, she seemed to bow her head to hide her charms. Physically, she retired into her own shell. But above all she was no longer her own mistress —she had already given herself, consecrated herself

to her hopes and aspirations. All she wanted was
the happiness of others. The real events of her life
were the events of public life. The words Liberty,
Peace and Justice were to her living beings of flesh
and blood, beings whom she loved; to her they
were what her children's names are to a mother.
Her purest and most unsullied devotion was reserved
not for her nearest and dearest but, gushing from
the depths of her soul, it leapt into the air like a
fountain dropping its refreshing fragrance far and
wide.

To those who watched her life, she seemed to
be entirely oblivious of self and interested only in
the fate of others. She was roused from her dreamy
reserve and became animated only when she engaged
in political controversy. Then, at the risk of appear‹
ing a bluestocking, she would quote the example of
Rome and Sparta, and deaf to the teasing of those
about her, uplifted and logical, she would continue
in her sweet seductive tones to defend her faith
in the Golden Age to come.

．　　．　　．　　．　　．

Alas ! It was not long before her faith was sub‹
jected to rude assaults. The long truce which for
almost two years had allowed the Constituent
Assembly to organize the rule of Liberty in peace,

had come to an end just about the time she took up her abode in the Rue St. Jean. The King's flight and his arrest at Varennes marked the beginning of the end.

The news of these two events reached Caen on the 23rd and 25th of June, 1791, and produced widespread disturbances, reviving the excesses and feverish excitement that had characterised the out-break of the Revolution. Men and women were again forced to hoist the tricolour in the streets, while in the country districts the peasants plundered the châteaux, the inmates of which had to seek refuge in the town.

In Caen itself there was a general atmosphere of excitement—drums beat, bells pealed joyfully or sounded the tocsin, and artillery salvoes and alarm signals were fired. In the evening everybody fell on each other's necks to the accompaniment of fire-works and illuminations, which were more or less compulsory. Disturbances were due mainly to the enforcement of the new clergy law. The constitu-tional priests, who had taken the oath, and the refractory priests, who had refused to do so, kept their own flocks and the two parties were constantly coming into conflict.

Sometimes there was hand-to-hand fighting, as happened during the outbreak which was long known in Caen as the affair of the 5th of November.[12] On that day the refractory curé of St. Jean had announced that he would say Mass at nine o'clock in the morning, and both sides gathered in front of the church; they insulted each other and soon shots were fired. The dead and wounded were picked up, the drums beat the alarm, panic spread through the town, and the rumour gained ground that there was a counter-revolutionary plot. The National Guard arrested over eighty supporters of the refractory priest and shut them up in the Château.

The affair of the 5th of November made all the deeper impression on Charlotte, since several of the prisoners were connected with her friends. Among them were some of the Achards and Levaillants.

She was also very much upset by the Verson incident which took place a month later. She knew this village, where her aunt had a house, very well, and she wrote to Mademoiselle Levaillant[13] that " every possible abomination " had been committed in Verson. Here again it was a matter of arresting priests, who had not taken the oath, and were guilty of having celebrated Mass. Some of the National Guard, taking guns from the Château, had placed themselves in charge of the expedition. But they arrived too late—the culprits had fled.

The troops, however, sacked the presbytery and looted the houses. They outraged women, including the curé's sister and the canon's mother, cutting off their hair with their swords and in some cases making notches in their foreheads. Barefooted and covered with blood, the unfortunate women were tied to the guns and brought to Caen during the night together with other prisoners. They were forced to carry torches and now and again their guards would seize hold of a torch and burn off any hair that still seemed too long. Three of these women died a few days later.

The expedition had been under the command of Gabriel de Cussy, the new commander of the National Guard. He was the man who, as deputy in the Constituent Assembly, had announced to his fellows the great news of the 4th of August with delirious enthusiasm, and caught up in the terrible competition, outdid himself so as not to be outdone by others. He had kept in step with the Revolution.

.   .   .   .   .

Charlotte became perturbed and alarmed. Such scenes shook her faith. Was it necessary for the great fight for liberty to involve such abominable excesses? Were they the price to be paid for the promised reign of bliss? Her fears were as yet

confusedly floating in her mind. But they first
became clearly defined when she found them form‐
ally and explicitly stated in a document given to her
for perusal by Augustin Leclerc.

It was an open letter addressed by his beloved
Abbé Raynal to the Constituent Assembly. A
secretary had read it aloud from the rostrum and
had been met with howls of fury and indignation
from members of the advanced parties.

Nevertheless, the scruples of this old octogenarian
were pathetic and worthy of all respect. He had
worked with the forerunners of the Revolution,
which was to a certain extent his own work, and
when he saw it descending to bloodshed he won‐
dered whether he were not partly responsible. " All
my life I have meditated over the ideas which you
have just applied to the regeneration of the king‐
dom, and I did so at a time when they represented
merely a pious wish. . . . Is it possible that I am
one of those who in expressing justifiable indigna‐
tion against arbitrary power have placed weapons
in the hands of license ? "

Perceiving the danger more clearly than others,
he claimed the right to raise the alarm. " Ready
as I am to descend into the shadow of the grave
and to leave that huge family whose welfare I have
so ardently desired, what do I see around me ?

D

Religious disturbances, civil strife, a Government enslaved to the tyranny of the mob ! "

He denounced the all-powerful influence of the Clubs, those writers " who profane the name of patriot ". And he pointed a warning finger at the Empires that had perished in anarchy, ending up with this last word of advice: " It is high time to restore confidence and peace."

How often Charlotte must have pondered this solemn adjuration ! Thus the last of the Encyclo-pædists, one of those who had prepared and given birth to the Revolution, was trembling for its fate, seeing it menaced on all sides, and compromised by its very excesses. He had sounded the alarm and demanded Peace !

CHAPTER III

MARAT

IT WAS not long before two tragedies enacted at the same moment and due to the same disturbing elements increased Charlotte's distress and anxiety. In Caen, the Deputy Attorney-General, Bayeux, was murdered in circumstances similar to those attending the assassination of Henri de Belzunce, but with possibly even greater cruelty, and in Paris the unpardonable September massacres took place.

On the 16th of August, 1792, the news had just reached Caen that the Tuileries had been captured and the Royal Family shut up in the Temple, when the rumour spread through the town that Monsieur Bayeux, the Deputy Attorney-General, had been arrested. Formerly Necker's secretary, and a lawyer of repute, he was a gentle, refined man, upright and cultured; he had published various essays and had translated Ovid.

The charge brought against him was not stated. The revolutionaries accused him of carrying on a correspondence with the *émigrés* while in the opposite camp it was declared that certain depart‹ mental officials, whose malpractices he had denounced, had sworn to have their revenge. His wife made up her mind to save him. Although she was expecting to become a mother at any moment, she set out for Paris, laid her case before the authorities, proved her husband's innocence and brought back an order for his release. The post took two days to reach Caen from Paris. Madame Bayeux performed the journey in fifteen hours. Arriving during the night of the 5th—6th of September, she secured a promise that the prisoner would be set free on the morning of the 6th.

But circumstances favoured her enemies. The Revolution was menaced on all sides; the rulers of Prussia and Austria, in alliance with the *émigrés*, were pushing forward with their troops to the frontiers. The Legislative Assembly, which had taken the place of the Constituent, had " declared war on Kings and peace for the peoples ". On all sides guns sounded the alarm, drums beat the call to arms, there were levies, appeals, and enrolling of recruits " to save the country from danger ".

But at the end of August it was learnt that the enemy forces had taken Longwy and were menacing Verdun. There was an immediate cry of panic:

" We have been betrayed ! " Mad with hatred, and imagining that conspiracy lurked at every corner, the blind mob was ready for all manner of violence.

Paris set the example. On the 5th of September, Caen heard of the prison massacres. The first mad rush of the infuriated mob had been on the Prison de l'Abbaye, where refractory priests, royalist officers and conspirators, and suspects were killed by hundreds, either put to the sword or shot. And the stream of blood spread from prison to prison. Thieves and pickpockets were killed, vagabonds and old men, ladies of rank and prostitutes, and even children who had been detained for correction. Beneath the Queen's windows in the Prison du Temple the rabid mob had displayed the dismembered remains of her friend, the gentle and retiring Princesse de Lamballe. Terrible scenes of pillage, rape and cannibalism had accompanied this orgy of blood.

With the news of these atrocities a circular also reached Caen from the Supervisory Committee of the Commune, calling upon the provinces to follow the example set by Paris. " The Paris Commune hastens to inform its brethren in the departments that a number of the ferocious conspirators detained in prison have been put to death by the people. This was an act of justice indispensable for terrorising traitors into keeping within bounds. Doubtless the whole nation will hasten to adopt similar measures so necessary for the public safety."

All the enemies of the Deputy Attorney-General eagerly spread this incredible call to crime through the town with the object of making Bayeux the target for a murderous assault; and consequently on the 6th of September, a mob drunk with fury and lust for vengeance shouted death to the traitor when Bayeux, who had been set free, left the Château. Was he not one of the villians who was responsible for the defeat, and ought he not to expiate his crime?

Bayeux understood. But he remained calm and collected. His little son of twelve came and flung himself in his arms, handing over to him the jewellery he was wearing and begging him to flee. But the mob was already surging towards him. He received a bayonet wound in the back and a bullet in the head and sank down on the front door-step of a house. The door was half open. He might have been saved. But a servant shut it in his face. And thus he died. A drum-major named Briant slashed his cheeks savagely with his sword; others cut off his head and carried it round the town on the end of a stick.

.   .   .   .   .

The September massacres, of which the murder
of Bayeux was but a bloodstained reflection, had
filled Charlotte with horror and despair.

Several of her friends who had been shut up in
the Château on the 5th of November, and then
transferred to the Paris prisons, had probably
perished in the horrible carnage. But it was not
the thought of these personal losses that tortured
her so much as the fact that the Revolution had
been deep dyed in blood. The disgust she felt
was as great as if she herself had been sullied by it.

There was one man who in her eyes had been
responsible for spreading the madness and unchain-
ing the bestial fury of the mob. There was one man
who had raised the cry for murder and filled the
ignorant masses with fanatical zeal. There was
one man who had let loose the forces of disrup-
tion and designated the victims. His name was
Marat.

She knew it. A few days before the massacres,
this man Marat had demanded them in his newspaper " L'Ami du Peuple. " He had written,
" The wisest plan would be to go fully armed to
the Abbaye, seize the traitors . . . and put them
to the edge of the sword."

She knew it ! The circular from the Commune
urging the provinces to follow the example set by

Paris and thus drown France in blood had been inspired by Marat, signed by Marat.

How could she possibly be ignorant of these communications ? Did she not read half a dozen political journals, Perlet's " Gazette " and Poncelin's " Gazette," Husson's " Courier " and Gorsas' " Courier," and Brissot's " Patriot " ? And had she not still her usual sources of information ?

True, in September, 1792, Gustave Doulcet, who had been elected deputy to the Convention, was preparing to leave for Paris. But she still had her friend Bougon-Longrais, who had succeeded the ill-fated Bayeux as Deputy Attorney-General, and would thus be in a position to follow events more closely than ever. Last, but not least, close behind her in the background, the faithful Augustin Leclerc, ever active, alert and vigilant, kept watch and ward. They both harboured the same hopes and deplored the same excesses. They hated the same monsters and revered the same deities. Sympathising alike in the things they loved and the things they hated, they lent each other fortitude and strength.

In Charlotte's mind there was thus no room for doubt. Marat was certainly the man responsible for the September massacres. His hands were red with blood. As a matter of fact, until then he had

hardly attracted her attention. She knew that for
three years his journal, "L'Ami du Peuple," had
been one long shriek of denunciation—The great
betrayal! The great plot! The great conspiracy!
And she remembered a panicky pamphlet: "We
are done for!" circulated at the time of the joyful
celebration of the Fêtes de la Fédération in 1790,
in which Marat demanded five hundred heads to
secure the happiness, peace and liberty of the
people. A year later, he suggested that La Fayette
and Bailly should have their throats cut, and that
the members of the Constituent Assembly, who had
sold themselves to the Court, should be impaled
and their mangled remains fastened to the battle-
ments of the hall to inspire terror in their suc-
cessors.

She imagined him misshapen and hideous, living
in a cave like an owl in its hole, and coming out
only to cry havoc and murder in the Jacobins' Club
or the Cordeliers' Club. In short, she had a confused
picture of him as a wild unbalanced fanatic, a
monster. It was only after the prison massacres
that for the first time he appeared to her in the
light of a tragic figure.

From that moment she scented her quarry and
concentrated her whole attention upon him. She
kept watch on him and followed his movements

on the political stage, while the great revolutionary drama continued to be unfolded.

.　　　.　　　.　　　.　　　.

The course of events soon brought her a fresh proof of Marat's responsibility. The publicist, the Club orator, the commissary of the Commune, had just been elected deputy to the Convention. On the 21st of September, 1792, the new Assembly had pro‹ claimed the Republic, and on the 25th it turned in a body with raised fists against "the friend of the people". One of the deputies accused him of having provoked the massacres and of aspiring to the dictatorship. Even Robespierre and Danton disavowed him. He got up on to the rostrum. "In this assembly I have a large number of personal enemies . . . " he began, but was interrupted by cries of "All of us ! All of us ! " Calm and collected, he tried to proceed, but the deputies sprang to their feet and overwhelmed him with abuse. "Get down ! Get down ! To the Abbaye !—To the guillotine ! "

But the fellow persisted and held his own. "Yes," he declared, "sometimes a dictatorship is neces‹ sary." And he proceeded to justify the massacres: "The people, obedient to my voice, saved the country by appointing themselves to the dictator‹

ship to get rid of the traitors." As the uproar continued, he brandished a pistol and held it to his
temple. He would kill himself at the foot of the
rostrum if they persecuted him! In disgust, the
Assembly proceeded with the business in hand,
showing their disapproval by contempt. Charlotte
could not forget this silent verdict.

.   .   .   .   .

She watched Marat during the trial of Louis XVI
before the Convention in January, 1793. She certainly had no sentimental feeling for the King or
for monarchy, and in the political controversies into
which she plunged from time to time, she passed
rigorous judgment on them in true Corneillian
style. " A feeble King cannot be good. . . . Kings
are made for the peoples, and not the peoples
for the Kings." Nevertheless, the execution of
Louis XVI, seemed to her a futile piece of cruelty,
a symbol of those excesses which in her eyes had
marred the Revolution, whose radiant features she
had seen shining through the night of the 4th of
August.

A number of deputies, while voting for the death
sentence on principle, wanted to avoid the execution
of the King, some moved by the fear of making him
a martyr, others solely out of humanity. Many of

the moderates, the Girondists, suggested an appeal to the people, who alone could grant him pardon. But Marat, following the example of the other Montagnards, acrimoniously opposed the suggestion, and demanded the King's head. Before the trial opened, he wrote in his journal: " I shall not believe in the Republic until the head of Louis XVI is no longer on his shoulders." And during the course of the debates he further insisted: " There will be no security, no peace, until the tyrant's head has fallen." By a small majority of 387 votes to 334, the King's execution was decided upon.

Charlotte was distressed beyond measure. She trembled for the future and for the peace of her country. " I shudder with horror and indignation," she wrote to her friend Rose Fougeron. " The most horrible things that can possibly be imagined lie in a future inaugurated by such happenings. . . . All these men, who ought to give us liberty, have killed her. They are nothing but common executioners." And, in her eyes, the chief of them was Marat.

·   ·   ·   ·   ·

She was still on the watch when, on the 12th of April, 1793, the Convention again turned on Marat. Was he not responsible for having unloosed the disturbances and encouraged the scenes of pillage which had horrified Paris at the end of February? Had he not actually encouraged rebellion against the Assembly?

This was perfectly true. As he had done in the case of the September massacres, Marat maintained that the people "despairing of an Assembly that encourages crime by allowing it to go unpunished," had been obliged to save themselves. On the very morning of these disturbances, he had written in his journal, which was now called "Le Journal de la République", "We must not think it strange that the people, driven to despair, should take justice into their own hands. In every country where 'the rights of the people' is not a mere empty phrase, the looting of a few shops and the hanging of a few monopolists on their doors would put an end to fraud and embezzlement."

Moreover, as President of the Jacobins, he had signed an appeal for revolt against the Assembly. "Yes, the counter-revolution is in the Government, in the National Convention! It is there you should strike! To arms, to arms, Republicans!"

Once again, obstinate and imperturbable, Marat held his ground. And he signed approval when the Girondist Guadet, read from the rostrum the appeal to insurrection launched by the Jacobins. "Yes! That's true! I agree!"

But his very calmness aroused the indignation of the Assembly. Pétion, usually so level-headed, inveighed against " the vile scoundrel who preaches despotism ", against the sort of man who was constantly urging the people to revolt. When the people had risen, what would there be to overthrow, what would there be left to kill ?

Boyer-Fonfrède urged the Convention to banish from its bosom " this malignant genius, this manufacturer of crime, calumny, trouble, discord and hatred. " Buzot was even more vehement: " The departments will bless the day when you deliver the human race from a man who is a disgrace to it, who has debased public morality, whose soul is full of calumny, and whose whole life is a tissue of crimes."

This time Marat avoided histrionics and did not point a pistol to his temple. The Assembly voted for his indictment. But the excited public immediately raised loud cries of protest from the galleries. They were beginning to interfere more and more in the debates, alternately cheering and hooting. More than once some of the deputies had endeavoured to take severe measures against their outbursts. Marat was the idol of these fanatics. On the present occasion they came down into the body of the hall and surrounded " the friend of the people ", and taking him under their protection, fought tooth and nail against his arrest.

Furthermore, when he appeared as a prisoner before the revolutionary Tribunal, Montané, the President, Fouquier-Tinville, the Public Prosecutor, judges and jury were on his side. He himself conducted the sitting, which was a mere formality, and was acquitted.

The mob surging about the walls of the Palais de Justice greeted him with a unanimous shout of welcome, crowned him with oak and laurel, and singing and dancing carried him in triumph to the Convention. Bare-armed, bristling with pikes and with Phrygian caps on their heads, the people filed in procession past the silent Assembly. A sapper, named Rocher, brandishing a hatchet, declared at the bar that his head would have to fall before a hair of " the friend of the people " was touched. From the rostrum Marat proclaimed his innocence and tasted the joy of apotheosis.

.   .   .   .   .

From the day on which he made his triumphal entry into the Convention on the shoulders of the mob, he continued to rise to ever loftier heights. In the Assembly he had his partisans, the Maratists. In the mouth of his enemies the epithet was a term of abuse. But he was proud of it: " It will become a title of honour," he declared, " for unless a man is a Maratist, it is impossible for him to be a tried patriot, a real defender of the people, a martyr of liberty." Thenceforward he posed as the great accuser before the Commune, the Cordeliers and even the Convention. He had reached the height of his glory.

Charlotte, who had been following his astonishing rise, was indignant and perturbed. The higher Marat soared, the more she hated him. And now he literally haunted her. She lived with his detested figure ever before her eyes.

During the seven months she had been secretly following his trial, she thought she had learnt to know him well. A description of him by Vergniaud, the most eloquent of the Girondists, rang continu͵ ally in her ears: " Marat, dripping with calumny, gall and blood, and raising his impudent head above the laws. " This was the picture she had formed of him.

In appearance he was a monster—short and squat, with a huge head, a quick jerky walk, dirty eccentric clothes, his forehead wrinkling under a red cap or a knotted handkerchief, his hooked nose squashed down over his large thin͵lipped mouth, his expres͵ sion insolent or sardonic, his complexion ashy grey and his eyes round, pale and restless, with whites of a greyish yellow.

In mind too he was a monster, eaten up with vanity and ambition, with vanity above all. Unap- preciated both as a scientist and doctor of medicine, as well as a philosopher and writer, all the books and memoirs he had published had served no purpose, but now at last, thanks to the Revolution, he had won the popularity he had been coveting for twenty years. Thenceforward he could not do without it. It was as much a necessity as the air he breathed. Arousing the lowest instincts of the ignorant mob, breathing hatred and suspicion into them day by day, and spewing his bitter and ferocious humour over them, he infected them with his own fever and delirium. But they continued to acclaim him !

Everything about him irritated Charlotte—the title of " doctor of incurables ", which he boasted of having received when he was still in practice, the name he had assumed and by which he signed himself, " Marat, the friend of the people ", as though he were *par excellence* the one and only friend of the people, as though he were exercising a privilege !

And had he not seized another monopoly, was he not giving lessons in patriotism to every French-

E

man, he, the man born in Prussian territory, of a
Swiss mother by a Sardinian father of Spanish
extraction? It was unheard of! And Charlotte
smiled bitterly at his insufferable arrogance. For
she had a sense of irony.

But, it might be urged, he was clear-sighted on
occasion. Good God! He spent his whole time in
denunciation! He was glued to the tocsin! His
journal and his pamphlet were one long screech
of alarm: "We are being lulled to sleep! Beware!
It is all a beautiful dream. The awakening will be
terrible." And if a man did wrong, how could
Marat fail to have prophesied it, seeing that he
was for ever accusing everybody of every sin under
the sun?

But, it might be further urged, as a man who was
one of nature's failures, was he not all the better
fitted to sympathise with the sufferings of the humble
and to feel the eternal injustice of which they were
the victims? He was sincere; more important still,
he was disinterested. What matter? He was
utterly detestable.

But the sin for which Charlotte could not forgive
him was his constant cry for blood. Of course he
tried to justify himself! The sooner the Revolution
was completed, the sooner would security and
happiness be restored. "With sword and burning

torch in hand we must expedite matters. . . . We spill blood so that no more need be spilt." The eternal refrain that keeps men in a state of war !

As early as the rejoicings in celebration of the Fêtes de la Fédération Marat had given vent to his discordant cries and demanded five hundred heads. In September, 1792, at the Conseil de la Commune, he had declared that the lives of forty thousand people were required to secure the public peace. Six weeks later, he wrote in his journal : " The machine will never work until the people have demanded justice of two hundred thousand scoundrels."

Thus his insensate demands increased year by year. Where would he stop ? Clearly he was the man who was keeping confusion and disorder alive and prolonging the strife. He was the very incarnation of evil, hatred and war. If he were removed, Peace would once again raise her head.

CHAPTER IV

THE AFFAIR OF THE 31ST OF MAY

THUS Charlotte kept her eyes steadily fixed on Paris. Meanwhile, during the month of April, 1793, in which Marat's triumph had been complete, a local event, the trial of the Abbé Gombault, attracted and held her attention, providing a further example of those revolutionary excesses which marred her ideal and filled her with shame and indignation.

On the 2nd of April, the Departmental Directorate had registered a decree of the Convention dealing with refractory priests, whereby all such men who were found on French soil a week after the promulgation of the law were to be punished with death.

The Abbé Gombault, ex-curé of St. Gilles, was arrested on the 3rd near la Délivrande, and a tribunal consisting of officers of the National Guard, immediately tried him. Several of them spoke in defence of the prisoner; the law, which only came into force a week after its promulgation, had not been registered till the day before and had not yet been posted. Nevertheless, after much paindul dis׳ cussion, the ex׳curé of St. Gilles was condemned to death, and on the 5th the guillotine was set up in the Place St. Gilles.

The new machine still aroused base curiosity. Adopted by the Legislative in March, 1792, it had been used for the first time in Caen in the November of that year under particularly atrocious circum׳ stances. In the suburb of Vauxcelles a couple named Delorme had killed their drunken neighbour in a brawl. The mob demanded their immediate trial, and when they were condemned to death insisted upon execution at once. In their impatience to see the guillotine working, they forced the executioner, in spite of his reluctance, to set up the machine and a cutler to sharpen the knife. In vain did the court object that the two Delormes had appealed against the sentence. The menacing mob would not listen. The judges, to protect themselves, persuaded the two prisoners to abandon their appeal. Dressed in red smocks, they were both executed, although the wife offered to die first in the hope that her husband would be reprieved.

Since this first execution, the Abbé Gombault had by the irony of fate frequently accompanied condemned prisoners to the guillotine, and as he walked to his own death, he was apparently less

moved than when he was helping and encouraging
others. Deep in prayer, he slowly mounted the steps
of the scaffold as though they were the steps of the
altar.

But the mob had tasted blood and wanted more.
On the pretext that it was impossible to put a worthy
curé to death and leave filthy rascals alive, they
rushed to the prisons, where they seized five prisoners,
murderers and thieves awaiting execution. As a
matter of fact, only four had been condemned to
death, and even they were appealing. The fifth
had been sentenced to twenty years in the galleys.
But the mob took no notice of such niceties, and
revelled in five executions.

.   .   .   .   .

Charlotte had followed the lightning trial of the
Abbé Gombault with passionate attention. Her
interest in it was all the greater since she knew one
of the judges, the brewer Lacouture, a major in the
National Guard, and one of those who had most
courageously pleaded in favour of the prisoner. He
was her next-door neighbour, his house being
situated just at the back of Madame de Bretteville's,
and separated from it only by a narrow courtyard
on to which one of Charlotte's two windows looked
out. She often used to sit there listening to Lacouture's sons playing the violin in the evening.

She blamed the " Marat faction " for inspiring these cruel laws, declaring that they were responsible for prolonging the disturbances and spreading an atmosphere of terror, bloodthirstiness and con‹ tagious madness throughout the country. And her circle shared her opinion. The " Marat faction " ! This was the name now given in the provinces to the most violent party in the Convention. And in the eyes of these distant spectators Marat was the leader.

The hideousness of his person, the studied untidiness of his dress, and the denunciatory fury of his language and his journal, all focused attention upon him. He stood out conspicuous, and from a distance hid the inhuman figures of two men who, as a matter of fact, were more powerful than he, the one riotous and rowdy and the other cold as ice— Danton and Robespierre.

No ! Charlotte was not the only one to curse Marat and his crew. Even those of her friends who were in official positions, like Bougon‹Longrais, publicly denounced these factionaries. Since the beginning of the year, the public bodies established in the department had on three different occasions sent solemn Addresses to the Convention, accusing " a handful of scoundrels, impudent agitators and bloodthirsty monsters of trying to intimidate the

Assembly and to perpetuate disorder and anarchy,"
and deploring the tyranny of the courts. Above
all they called upon the Convention to put an end
to the dissensions which were tearing and weakening
it and bringing disaster upon the country. They
all mentioned Marat by name.

These pathetic Addresses were full of allusions
borrowed from ancient history. Indeed, the Revolution had taken the Roman Republic, with its fierce
love of liberty, as its model, and the glory of ancient
Rome even influenced their mode of expression.
The authors of these proclamations extolled the
heroic determination of Mucius Scaevola and
expressed abhorrence of the crimes of a Catiline
"Let us be Catos!" they adjured the deputies,
"otherwise we shall be men like Brutus!"

So, by a curious coincidence, these men spoke
the language which the great-grand-daughter of
Corneille had learnt in the Presbytery of Vicques,
in the works of her illustrious ancestor. Thus it
was all the more comprehensible to her. Their
hatred of Marat inflamed her own, and her heart
was bursting at the thought of all the prosecutions.

These struggles, which the magistrates of Clavados
deplored in their Addresses, brought the Montagnards and the Girondists to grips in the very heart
of the Convention. The nickname of Montagnards

had at first been given as a joke to the blood-and-thunder deputies who occupied the raised seats to the left of the President. They had accepted it and made it their emblem. They were determined to push the Revolution to the utmost lengths, and to rid it of all its enemies, both inside and outside the Convention. And they maintained that violence was inevitable.

There had already existed in the Legislative Assembly a group of deputies from the south-west, the Gironde, and its numbers had been increased in the Convention. Although from this time onwards they were recruited from all over the country, they continued to be known as the Girondists. They held the reins of power and their aim was to put bounds to the Revolution and organize peace.

Between the Montagnards and the Girondists there lay the Plain or the Marsh, an inert, amorphous mass, hurled from one side to the other, like badly trimmed ballast at the mercy of the hurricane.

Separated less by doctrine than by the means whereby they hoped to achieve success, the Girondists and the Montagnards tore each other to pieces. It was the everlasting conflict between the partisans of reform and the upholders of violence. The Girondists accused the Montagnards of pushing the country towards dictatorship or anarchy, while the Montagnards declared that the Girondists were federalists. Owing to constant misuse, the word had changed its meaning. The impressive festivals of 1790, celebrating the touching union of the provinces, the Fédération, were a long way off. According to the Montagnards, the Girondists were aiming at creating provincial republics and of dis-membering the country.

Apparently, the Girondists had no more rabid foe than Marat. To use Charlotte's expression, he was not only " the summit of the Mountain " he was also the adored orator of the howling, raving benches. He was the mouthpiece of even more rabid external forces whose tone he was obliged to adopt if he wished to remain their leader —the armed Sections, the Jacobins' Club and the Cordeliers' Club, and, above all, the Paris Commune.

Marat contemptuously called the Girondists " statesmen," implying that they were static men, and upbraided them for not being men of action. He accused them of being the harbingers of the counter-revolution, and pretended to believe they were the accomplices of General Dumouriez, the recent victor of Jemmapes and Valmy, who had just escaped abroad. He openly denounced them as traitors, who not only wished to dismember the country but also aimed at sending it to perdition.

Charlotte was a whole-hearted admirer of the Girondists. She loved their courage and generosity, their wit and eloquence. They were taunted with being somewhat poetical. But it was these poets who were the real founders of the Republic. Their ideal was her ideal. Moreover, she felt that a refined and resolute woman, Madame Roland, was guiding and sustaining them, animating them with her spirit and communicating to them her gentle enthusiasm, her humane reasonableness. Charlotte espoused their cause. They were her real heroes. All the abuse hurled at them by Marat fell upon her shoulders. And each of these blows tempered and retempered the blade of her loathing.

   .   .   .   .   .

Thus she trembled for the fate of the Girondists in this struggle in which she felt that no quarter would be given. But she certainly could not guess to what an impudent blow they would succumb.

It was Marat who delivered, guided and led this decisive assault. The drama was enacted during the two days of the 31st of May and the 2nd of June, but it was always known as the affair of the

31st of May. On the first day the action was unde-
cided, but at the beginning of the second day
events moved fast and furiously.

The 2nd of June was Marat's great day. Now
hidden in the background, now in full view, he was
here, there, and everywhere. It was he who ordered
the Tuileries, in which the Convention was sitting,
to be invested by the National Guard under the
command of Hanriot.

It was he who inspired and directed the deputa-
tion from the Commune which presented itself at
the bar of the Assembly and demanded the arrest
of some thirty Girondists. " Save the people," ran
the petition, " or we warn you that they will save
themselves ! "—Marat's favourite formula !

During the course of the session, it was he who
demanded the arraignment of the Girondists, while
they were hesitating and squabbling, some being
ready to resign " in order to restore peace to
the Republic ", others resolved to remain at their
posts.

Suddenly, some of the deputies came back into
the hall, defeated and furious, their clothes all torn.
Hanriot had forbidden them to leave the House.
The Assembly was no longer free ! It was surrounded
by troops. A voice was raised proposing that the
Convention should hold its deliberations outside

under the protection of the armed forces that were there. In spite of hoots and shouts of " To arms ! " raised from the benches, the deputies filed out, led by their President, Hérauldt de Séchelles.

But in the Cour de la Carrousel, Hanriot, who was on horseback, hurled himself upon the proces⁄sion. He was supported by thousands of armed men, and a hundred and fifty guns ready to fire. The President ordered him to let them pass. " You are not here to give orders," shouted Hanriot in thundering tones, drawing his sword and bringing it down on his adversary's hat. " We are not here to listen to words but to seize the traitors. To your guns, you fellows ! "

All the exits from the garden were barred, and from one of them Marat emerged, escorted by a band of young guttersnipes. " In the name of the people, I order you to return to the posts you have so basely abandoned ! " he roared. The Montagne group re⁄entered the building. The Plain and the Gironde followed in silence.

In the rear of the herd he had turned back, Marat entered as master and dictated his will. Adding a name here, crossing out another there, he drew up with his own hand a list of thirty⁄two deputies who were to be arrested. And he carried the vote in the midst of a terrific uproar, the crowds of petitioners

and people from the galleries mingling in the body
of the hall with the Montagnards.

.   .   .   .   .

It was on the 4th of June that the news of this
unprecedented *coup de force* reached Charlotte.
The Assembly had held its deliberations under
threat of the guns ! This meant the death blow
of National Representation, of Law, Liberty and
Peace. Marat was indeed sending the country head-
long towards limitless bloodshed. From that moment
she felt the idea quicken and leap to life within her
which for months, ever since September, had been
growing and developing in her mind. She must
kill Marat !

CHAPTER V

THE GIRONDISTS AT CAEN

THE AFFAIR of the 2nd of June had aroused violent indignation among the officials of Calvados, who had rallied almost unanimously to the support of the Girondists. As their Addresses to the Convention proved, they had fore‹ seen it some time previously.

Up to the last moment, they had endeavoured to prevent the outrage. During the night of the 30th—31st of May, they passed a decree in favour of raising an armed force strong enough, if the need arose, to protect the representatives of the nation. And they forthwith dispatched ten commissaries to Paris to inform the Convention of their decree. Their last Address ended with the following words: " We declare war to the death against anarchists, proscriptionists, and sedition‹mongers, and we shall not lay down our arms until we have reduced them to silence. " But the ten commissaries arrived too late. The drama was over.

In the eyes of the leading men of Normandy, the Convention, after the 2nd of June, was invested and blockaded by the fanatics of the Commune, who blindly obeyed the behests of Marat. It was imperative to release it, and to secure the safety of its members and the freedom of its sessions.

On the 7th of June, the very day on which the ten commissaries reported the failure of their mission, all the official bodies and civic societies of Calvados laid the foundations of an Assembly appointed to resist oppression.

As he was ill, the Deputy Attorney-General, Bougon-Longrais, was obliged to be carried in an armchair to attend the first sitting. General de Wimpffen was entrusted with the task of raising volunteers. By a unanimous vote it was decided that the men should fraternise with the people of Paris who did not know what Marat and the Commune were aiming at. They would appear as saviours and set the Convention free by their mere presence. No blood would be shed.

Charlotte shared the indignation of Bougon-Longrais and his colleagues, but not their confidence. She did not think that the expedition would be such an easy matter, or assume the appearance of a triumphal march. She foresaw fresh hecatombs of victims and endless civil war. And she could not bear it.

Every time she heard the drums beat for the recruiting of volunteers, she felt the resolution, which had been formulated in her mind, gaining strength. To hasten the advent of peace and save the lives of thousands and thousands of men, she must kill Marat.

.   .   .   .   .

Suddenly, the rumour spread through the town that a large number of proscribed Girondists were making their way to Caen. From the commissaries sent to Paris and the deputies from Calvados they had learnt that, ever since the 31st of May, the capital of Normandy had become the centre of armed resistance to the Maratists, and they were hastening to place themselves under the protection of troops who would lead them back in triumph to Paris.

The Girondists were coming to Caen! It is almost impossible to imagine Charlotte's perturbation at the news. She was going to see the men for whose fate she had been trembling for months and whose defeat had strengthened her resolve !

About the heads of them all shone the halo of talent and courage, some of them were even crowned with glory. They were her heroes, her demi-gods ! They were the incarnation of her republican ideal

F

which they had defended without flinching at the risk of their lives. Were they not the most pitiful victims of Marat? Had he not denounced them as traitors? And would they not be even more exposed to his wrath now that they had entered into open rebellion against him? But she would save them, them and thousands of others! She would restore peace to them. At the thought her secret leapt in her bosom.

She was going to see them! They would be her neighbours! The Opposition Assembly had placed the old Hotel de l'Intendance at their disposal. It was in the Rue des Carmes, which ran into the Rue St. Jean opposite Madame de Bretteville's house. From the window of a little room next to the salon the Girondist quarters could be seen a hundred yards away, and from this place of observation Charlotte must often have watched the new inmates of the Intendance going in and out.

They began to arrive on the 9th of June, either in little groups or one by one. Some of them had succeeded in escaping from Paris only under cover of disguise. As soon as they arrived, they presented themselves before the Opposition Assembly, where they were content with giving a brief report of the political situation. A certain number of them stayed on for the sittings, but they rarely if ever spoke and never in public. Guided by a sort of tact in keeping with their character, they avoided intruding upon a movement which had been in existence before their arrival. They felt it should be left in the hands of the men who had been responsible for calling it into being.

Charlotte was so anxious to make their acquaintance that she contrived opportunities for meeting them. She went out more than usual and used to visit Monsieur Lévêque, the President of the Departmental Directorate. He held meetings in his house of sincere and enthusiastic Republicans who were opposed to the violence of the Maratists, and they were joined by some of the fugitives. She was present at the reviews when General de Wimpffen recruited volunteers from the ranks of the National Guard. She appeared at the meetings of the Opposition Assembly, in which the delegates of seven departments in Normandy and Brittany solemnly met to discuss the deliverance of the Convention.

On these occasions she would have one of those fits of coquetry to which she was always subject whenever she put on her best clothes. There was nothing slovenly about her now; she did not hang her head or let her chin fall on to her chest, nor did her skirts sweep the street. Once again she was the great lady who knew how to dress, and she recovered her charming air of queenly authority without sacrificing her sweetness and reserve.

At these gatherings, when she used to catch a glimpse of the Girondists without addressing them, she scrutinised them carefully, noting their looks and any details she could gather about their lives.

She saw Gorsas, the scathing journalist with the distorted features whose " Courrier des Départe‹ ments " she used to read ; Buzot, still overwhelmed by the recent arrest of Madame Roland, for whom he had a tender and passionate friendship ; Guadet, thin and dark, energetic and outspoken; Salles, who had three times courageously denounced Marat at a plenary session of the Convention; Louvet, pale and thin, witty and dapper, the success of whose novel " Faublas " had perhaps been responsible for arousing the hatred of Marat, whose failure in literature had made him jealous; Pétion, who in spite of his grey hair was a favourite with the ladies, Pétion, who had been so popular as Mayor of Paris, that after his suspension in 1792 the people clamoured for his return, shouting " Pétion or death ! "; and Barbaroux, bewildering in his youth and energy, fair as Adonis and endowed with all the gifts of the gods, who at the age of twenty‹six already knew both glory and shame.

She was so deeply preoccupied with these men that her letters to her father were full of descriptions of them. Occasionally, in spite of her admiration, the good-humoured irony which came naturally to her, would allow a malicious little touch to slip in.

.   .   .   .   .

At each of these encounters her excitement increased. The idea she had conceived had taken shape and its main outlines were already clear. She had made up her mind to kill Marat at a plenary session of the Convention; the crowds from the galleries, whose idol he was, would certainly swarm over the benches and kill her on the spot. No one would know her name.

She was ready. Death no longer frightened her. It was constantly being invoked. All the orators, on the slightest pretext, swore that they would die at their posts, and declared that they were ready to lay down their lives. Even the image of death had become familiar to her. In the streets of Caen she often saw the standard of a certain popular society known as the " Carabots ". They were somewhat rough and rowdy, but devoted to the Girondist cause. Above their device " The fulfilment of the Law or Death ", a skull and cross-bones were cut out in black on a white ground. The Carabots even wore amulets with the same sinister device, which had become quite familiar. They were right: "The fulfilment of the Law or Death!"

Charlotte, it is true, was filled with particular admiration for the stern manners and customs of Rome and Sparta, as revealed to her in the pages of history and tragedy. Did not her women friends chaff her for continually quoting them as examples? But she was not the only one to draw her inspiration from them. Everybody about her extolled the heroes of antiquity who were ever ready to kill or be killed in a great cause. Thus she was filled with wholehearted admiration for Brutus who sacrificed Cæsar to Liberty, although he was his benefactor and perhaps his father. She knew whole passages of Voltaire's "Brutus" by heart. But everybody held up Brutus as a model, and speeches and articles without end were inspired by the subject of his dagger.[14] He was, so to speak, raised aloft on the shoulders of the Age.

But Charlotte was even more deeply imbued than the rest with classic lore and felt as ready as the heroes of old to kill and be killed. Thenceforward she devoted herself heart and soul to the plan she had conceived. As it stirred to life in her breast, she lived for it and it alone. It invaded her entire being and occupied her whole mind. It became

the object of her life and of her thought. Inspired
by it, she went straight to her goal.

.   .   .   .   .

Yet there was a moment when she hesitated. As
soon as the opposition movement became clearly
defined in Normandy, the Convention despatched
emissaries charged with bringing back the lost
sheep to the fold. The first of these, who were sent
openly, Romme and Prieur, members of the Con≠
vention, were arrested on the 12th of June[15] and
kept as hostages in the Château. Whereupon secret
envoys, both men and women, were entrusted with
the task of propaganda. They mingled with the
crowd, obtained access to the houses, and insinuated
themselves into the confidence of their hosts. Their
activities even reached Charlotte.

They pointed out to the people of Normandy the
risks they ran in being treated as rebels and in
exposing themselves for the sake of a ruined party.
They disparaged the Girondists, declaring that they
were heroic but superficial, brilliant but lacking in
determination. They possessed the gift of eloquence
but had no political sense. They had taken part in
the Revolution involuntarily and without under≠
standing its object.

The emissaries from the Montagne contrasted
these misguided artists with men like Marat, for

they were well aware that all the hatred of the provinces was concentrated on him. And they defended him, forestalling the calumnies his enemies were spreading about him. Because, after having lived in England for ten years, he had grown accus= tomed to a certain degree of modest comfort, he was being accused of hiding a refined manner of life and a taste for luxury beneath an exterior of studied slovenliness. Even his violence served a salutary purpose, for every time the nation was tempted to stop half=way, he alone was capable of whipping it up and lashing it on towards the heights. His enemies also accused him of having a biting tongue. But gall was a necessary stimulant in a living body, and there were certain conditions in which it saved the entire organism. At heart Marat was good. When he was practising as a doctor, had he not time and again given his services for nothing to hundreds of penni= less patients ? He was filled with sincere love for the people, inspired thereto by a mother whom he adored. He had reached maturity to the accompani= ment of suffering, study and meditation, in which he had brought all his inflexible determination to bear. He was the nation itself ! He was the soul of the Revolution !

But Charlotte shook her head. No, no ! Marat did not love the people. To love the people could not mean rousing the worst instincts of the ignorant masses in order to remain their idol, and inciting them to butchery on pretext of saving them. To love the people meant restoring Peace.

All too long had she lent an ear to this servile adulation. More eager than ever to take action after this false alarm, she hastily returned to the path she had marked out for herself.

.   .   .   .   .

The plan she had nurtured in lonely secrecy now took definite shape. It was formed, so to speak, in her own image, with its practical common sense, its tincture of shrewd malice and all its great-hearted benevolence. It was to enable her to approach her heroes, to do a favour to one of her women friends and to be of service to her great cause.

She wanted to get an introduction through one of the Girondist refugees in Caen to a deputy who still kept his seat in the House and would help her to reach Marat in the very heart of the Convention. But whom was she going to choose among the eighteen refugees, and what pretext was she to give ?

Chance came to her help. She wanted to go to the Ministry of the Interior on behalf of her friend Mademoiselle de Forbin, who had taken refuge in

Switzerland, and she accidentally discovered that
the families of the Forbins and the Barbaroux, both
of which came from the south of France, were
connected by ties of friendship. Barbaroux was
obviously the man to help her in the matter.

Mademoiselle de Forbin, who had been canoness
in the Abbaye de Troarn near Caen, was entitled to
a pension after the suppression of the monastic
orders, but the Ministry had refused to grant it
on the ground that she was living abroad, and was
therefore an *émigrée*. Charlotte, who had taken her
friend's affairs in hand, thought she would have a
better chance of success if she applied to the local
government of Calvados. But she required the
papers which had been lying for months at the
Ministry, and had not succeeded in obtaining them.
If she went to Paris, she would take the opportunity
to get them herself. She would ask Barbaroux to
give her an introduction to one of his colleagues,
who would help her and guide her to the right
department.

Behind her, in the background, was a man who
shared her enthusiastic admiration for the Giron⸗
dists, who strongly encouraged her to see them and
offered to accompany her and protect her. It was
Augustin Leclerc. He had recently married, and
Charlotte had insisted on signing the marriage

register. But the change in his life had not made any difference to his relations with Madame de Bretteville and her niece. On the contrary, he was still the old lady's steward, and his young wife was also taken into her service.

Charlotte did not wish to deprive him of the pleasure of interviewing the Girondists, though she naturally told him nothing of her secret intentions. It was towards the end of June that they entered the gate of the Intendance with its iron carriage guards on either side.

The Opposition Assembly had given the Girondists a guard of honour, and, after showing Charlotte into the large salon on the ground floor, one of the men on duty had gone to inform Barbaroux of her arrival. This room had been dismantled for four years, but its finely carved panelling had been restored and it had been hastily furnished with a few chairs. Two deputies, who had been sitting in a corner, discreetly withdrew. They were Meillan and Guadet. Barbaroux did not keep her waiting long.

The interview was short. In her sweet musical voice, Charlotte referred to the ties they had in common, calmly made her request, telling him that she intended to obtain Mademoiselle de Forbin's papers, and asking for his help. The Girondist immediately suggested giving her an introduction to his friend Lauze de Perret, to whom he promised to write at once. He then conducted her to the door.

Augustin Leclerc gazed upon them in ecstasy. He had been accustomed to say " beautiful as Charlotte Corday ". He could now add " hand⁄some as Barbaroux ". And indeed they were an ideal couple; she, fair in the sunlight, with her dazzling complexion, her full figure, her reserved and queenly grace; he, dark and strong, with his leonine brow, his large deep⁄set eyes, flashing teeth and features of a classic purity that incipient corpu⁄ lence had softened without blurring.

A week later, the faithful Augustin Leclerc again accompanied Charlotte to the Intendance. Bar⁄ baroux had received no reply from Lauze de Perret. He was not surprised, as all correspondence was strictly censored. Neither was Charlotte perturbed. She told him that she had now made up her mind to go to Paris in any case, and that she would take his letter of introduction to Lauze de Perret herself, and offered to deliver any letters and papers that the Girondists in Caen wanted to reach their friends in Paris safely. The date of her departure, she added, was still uncertain.

Thus at the very beginning of July Charlotte had quite made up her mind to go to Paris. The offer to take the correspondence of the Girondists was a proof of it. She had given herself a fresh pledge of her resolution. Coquetry, which always played a part at great moments of her life, had also had its say, for she had already ordered a pair of high-heeled shoes for her journey to Paris.

. . . . . .

Meanwhile, the Opposition Assembly was endeavouring to extend its power. It sent out fiery proclamations couched in lurid terms addressed to the people of Calvados and the neighbouring departments, as well as to the rest of France. All these manifestos promised that the Convention would be delivered by a great fraternal sally on behalf of the people of Paris, and poured anathema on the heads of Marat and his followers.

The refugees were also working hard. In less than a month they sent out nine pamphlets from Caen. They did not openly make speeches, but discreetly supported the Opposition Assembly. On the 18th of June, Barbaroux had addressed a stirring manifesto to his fellow citizens in Marseilles: " Men of France, let us march on Paris, not to fight the people of Paris but to deliver them, and safeguard the unity of the Republic one and indivisible ! Let us march on Paris, not to dissolve the National

Convention but to set it free ! . . . Let us march on Paris to punish the assassins and hurl the dictators from the Tarpeian Rock ! ''

On the 30th of June, the day on which seven departments formed themselves into a Central Opposition Assembly, another manifesto was sent out from Caen. It was called Wimpffen's Manifesto, but, as a matter of fact, it had been drawn up by the Girondist Louvet. It denounced the misdeeds of the factionaries at great length, and demanded their punishment. '' They will be punished for the revolt of the 31st of May and the crime of the 2nd of June. They will be punished, because on those days, to the seditious sound of the tocsin, with a hundred parricidal guns, they gave orders for thirty-two deputies, against whom unfounded charges were brought, to be torn from their seats and held back with daggers at their throats. Lastly, they will be punished for having seized what they considered a favourable opportunity for making, through the instrumentality of the vilest of men, a first daring attempt to force the nation to accept a leader.''

In spite of all these appeals, volunteers did not present themselves in as large numbers as the Opposition Assembly could have wished. Yet the promised pay of two francs a day was a large sum for the period, and the leading men set the example.

Many of the Departmental officials declared themselves ready to go. Bougon-Longrais had enlisted
as early as the 12th of June. Shortly afterwards, it is
true, he was called upon to act as President of the
Opposition Assembly in the Eure district. Other
friends of Charlotte, such as the Abbé de Jumilly,
the constitutional curé of St. Jean, also figured
among the recruits.

A final effort to raise volunteers was made on
Sunday the 7th of July. On that day a grand
review,[16] announced by placards, summoned the
National Guard to assemble in the Cours-la-Reine.
Crowds collected. Speeches followed the parade and
the march past with bands playing. Finally, General
de Wimpffen, followed by several members of the
Central Assembly, went down the ranks to take the
names of volunteers. He succeeded in getting only
seventeen.

Charlotte was present at this review and occupied
a place near a group of Girondists who took no part
in the speech-making. She now knew most of them.
Pétion, always captivated by a beautiful face, noticed
her melancholy looks. "Would you be sorry if they
didn't go?" he asked her, thinking she had some
particular interest in one of the few volunteers who
had just enlisted.

She answered only by a vague gesture. Her

secret sealed her lips. She could not tell him how utterly mistaken he was. At the very moment he put his question she had just settled the one uncertain item in her plan—the date of her departure !

Her disappointment at the small number of volunteers made her all the more touched by the courage of those who had enlisted. She would spare them the fight ! What was the good of risking their young lives ? All that was required was for a woman's hand to put an end to civil war and restore Peace ! She would reach Paris before them and not postpone her departure any longer. The next diligence for Paris left Caen on the following Tuesday. She would take it.

On that very Sunday, immediately after the review, she went to the Intendance, and asked Barbaroux to prepare the letter of introduction to Lauze de Perret, and the correspondence she was to take. He promised to send them to her on the morrow. A number of the refugees had gathered together in the salon and were discussing the events of the day, affecting a confidence they were very far from feeling. Charlotte listened eagerly and even took part in their conversation. This was the last time she would see them before she saved them.

Just as she was taking her leave, Pétion came in, and still misled with regard to her, complimented

" the beautiful aristocrat who came to visit the Republicans". This time she did not altogether succeed in controlling herself. "You are judging me without knowing me, citizen Pétion," she replied. "One day you will know who I am!"

.   .   .   .   .

This was her worst slip of the tongue. During her last hours in Caen she did not always succeed in hiding the thought that was haunting her beneath her calm good cheer. But she never gave herself away any further.

On the Sunday evening, when she returned to Madame de Bretteville's, she stopped at Lunel's rooms on the ground floor. She used often to drop in, but on this occasion she was feverish and flustered. She described the review in the Cours-la-Reine to the carpenter and his wife. "No!" she cried, bringing down her hand on the table at which the couple were playing cards, "never shall it be said that Marat ruled France!"

And she spoke in much the same way when Madame de Bretteville found her in tears and cross-questioned her: "I am weeping for the misfortunes of my country, for my family and for you. As long as Marat is alive, who can be sure of life?"

Nor when she went to see her friend, Madame

G

Gautier de Villiers, at Verson, did she succeed in hiding her agitation, being alternately extremely communicative and absent-minded. The sweet harmony of her voice and gesture had vanished. Alas! The bonds that held her to life were beginning to be loosed. On her walk to Verson she trod for the last time the soil of her beloved Normandy, sweet with the scent of new-mown hay under the blue of the July sun, and for the last time drank in the breeze from the open country redolent of the salt of the sea and of all the flowers of the field.

On the other hand, nothing betrayed her agitation when she went to visit the gardens of the Chevalier de Longueville in the Fossés St. Julien, or when she took back some books to Madame de Pontécoulant, her old Abbess, who, since the closing of the convents, had been living in retirement with some of her nuns in the Place St. Sauveur.

She told most of her friends that she was shortly going to Argentan, where her father had been living since January. She had to give some explanation for the preparations she was making. She had foreseen everything, and made the most minute calculations. Step by step she carried out the plan she had conceived and for so long carried about with her in secret. It had now become, as it were, a living being, perfect and complete, born of her body, and remaining invisible beside her, taking her by the hand and leading her irresistibly on. She obeyed it like a mother who allows herself to be dragged on by her child.

On the morning of Monday, the 8th, she received the parcel Barbaroux had promised her, consisting of a sealed envelope, which no doubt contained the letter of introduction,[17] and the papers to be delivered to Lauze de Perret. The packet was accompanied by a note from Barbaroux begging her to keep him informed of her movements. She wrote to thank him and promised to give him news of her journey.

In the afternoon, in the intervals between paying visits, she settled a few small debts and booked a place in the diligence for the next day in her own name. She was ready ! She even had a passport.[18] She had had to procure one at the beginning of April to go to Argentan. And, at the end of that month, when she was accompanying one of her women friends to the passport office at the Town Hall she had taken the risk of having her own viséd for Paris.

In her own room she set to work to burn her newspapers, her pamphlets and letters, even to the last note from Barbaroux. As she was putting the papers on the fire the wail of a violin was wafted in through the open window opposite her own in the little courtyard. It was the violin played by the Lacouture brothers, to which she had so often listened in the evening during the last two years. She would never hear it again!

On the morning of Tuesday, the 9th, she wrote to her father. Her tale to all her friends was that she was going to pay him a visit, but she wrote to him that she was going to England where her uncle, the Abbé de Corday, had already sought refuge.

" Although I owe you obedience, my dear father," she wrote, " I am going away without your permission and without seeing you, because it would give me too much pain. I am going to England because I do not think it is possible to live in peace and happiness in France for long. I am posting this letter just before leaving, and when you receive it I shall no longer be in this country. . . . "

She said good-bye to Madame de Bretteville, who was also under the impression that she was going to Argentan. It was a trying ordeal. She was bound to the kind old lady by all the ties of intimacy and gratitude. Had not Augustin Leclerc informed her that her aunt had made a will in her favour and left everything to her? She might have posed as a rich heiress in the town!

But probably the person from whom she found it most difficult to hide her secret was Augustin Leclerc. Had he not enlightened her? Had they not vied with each other in love for the real Revolution, admiration for the Girondists, and, above all, hatred of Marat? But she had promised herself not to reveal her secret to anyone. And she would keep her word.

From her room she could see little Louis Lunel, the carpenter's son, in the inner courtyard. She called out to him, and descending the narrow winding stone stairs for the last time, gave the child some of her drawings and a pencil-box: "Be a good boy," she said. "And give me a kiss."

But Azor, the little dog belonging to the house, tried to follow her. In the alley leading to the Rue St. Jean, Ninette, the cat, was prowling. She loved them both and gently caressed them. They were the only creatures to whom she had not been obliged to lie on taking leave of them for ever!

CHAPTER VI

THE MURDER

CHARLOTTE had promised Barbaroux to send him details of her journey, and she kept her word. We have her own description. But the tale of her adventures is extremely brief, for she dozed most of the way in the diligence, in which about ten passengers were packed in the appalling heat. " She might almost say she woke up only when she reached Paris."

As soon as they started, her travelling companions began to talk politics. As they were Montagnards, their discussions, " which were as stupid as their persons were disagreeable ", helped to send her to sleep. But one of the passengers, " who doubtless liked women when they were asleep", took or pretended to take her for the daughter of one of his old friends, and calling her by a name she had never heard, ended by offering her his name and his fortune.

" We are playing a regular comedy," she told him at one of the posting-houses, when his importunacy was becoming tiresome. "It is unfortunate that so much talent should not have an audience. I am going to fetch our fellow travellers so that they may share the entertainment."

He took the hint and stopped his play-acting, confining himself during the night to murmuring plaintive ditties "which were extremely soporific in their effect". But on nearing Paris she was again subjected to his unwelcome attentions, and was obliged to refuse him her own and her father's address. For he was determined to ask her hand in marriage.

.   .   .   .   .

Charlotte had never been to Paris. She had a few acquaintances there who might have helped her to find her way about. But she was determined to be independent of everybody and to act on her own initiative. She had not told anyone that she was coming, and there was nobody waiting to meet her when, at about midday on Thursday, the 11th, the diligence drew up in the courtyard of the Messageries Nationales in the Rue Notre-Dame-des-Victoires.

In accordance with her pre-arranged plan, she made enquiries at the office, asking to be recom- mended a hotel in the neighbourhood, and an official gave her a card with the address, " Madame

Grollier, proprietress of the Hôtel de la Providence, 19, Rue des Vieux Augustins, near the Place de la Victoire,Nationale. Furnished rooms at all prices. Paris."

Without troubling to search further, she followed a commissionaire who carried her scanty luggage. The proprietress, Madame Grollier, cross,questioned her fairly closely, to make sure she would not be doing anything to get herself into trouble with the police, who were extremely exacting and vigilant, and also to satisfy her own curiosity.

On learning that Charlotte came from Caen, she asked her whether it was true that an armed force was marching on Paris. Anxious at all costs to escape being regarded as a suspicious character, Charlotte put her off the scent, merely describing the recruiting that had taken place on the 7th of July, and assuring her landlady "that there were not thirty people in the square in Caen when the drums beat the call for recruits to go to Paris."

She was taken to room number 7 on the first floor front. It was a fairly large room with red and white curtains, and contained, in addition to the bed and some chairs, a chest of drawers and a small writing, table. Charlotte was tired and was longing to lie down. But she asked the waiter to buy her some paper, pens and ink. And while he was making the bed, she asked him what people in Paris thought of Marat. He replied that the aristocrats hated him, but that patriots regarded him as a good citizen. She smiled ironically.

But, as he went on with his work, the man told her that unfortunately Marat was prevented from attend, ing the Convention as he was ill and had been obliged to stay at home for some weeks.

He little guessed what his information meant to Charlotte. What a revelation! She suddenly dis, covered that since the 31st of May she had ceased to follow Marat's movements and to keep watch on his words and actions. On that date she had passed her verdict on him. She had been entirely absorbed in the arrival of the Girondists in Caen and the preparations for her plan, and knew nothing about Marat's illness and his absence from the Assembly. Thus it was impossible for her to carry out her plan as she had arranged—to kill Marat in the very heart of the Convention and perish at the hands of the mob in the galleries, without leaving her name or any trace of her identity, while all those who knew her would think she was in England.

But Marat had to be killed and Peace restored to the country! It was absolutely necessary! So, in spite of her fatigue, she thought out a fresh plan. Since he was confined to his house, she would kill him there. She now had no need of Lauze de Perret to obtain access to the Convention. But she had to see him to give him the papers from Barbaroux and settle Alexandrine de Forbin's business. She would do this immediately.

She therefore changed her mind and told the waiter she would not go to bed at once. She wanted to go out for a little while and see the Palais Royal, and she asked him casually to tell her the way to the Rue St. Thomas-du-Louvre, where Lauze de Perret lived.

It was quite close to her hotel, but his two daughters informed Charlotte that their father had been kept at the Convention and had not yet come in. So she left the parcel from Barbaroux and said she would come back for an answer in an hour's time.

Then she wandered about. It was the hottest time of day, and the city seemed to be dozing. She was not surprised to find everything so calm and quiet in these troublous times. In Caen she had often seen everything going on as usual when there was rioting a few yards away. She could not bring herself to take any interest in the sights or even in the public buildings. She was obsessed with her own thoughts.

When she returned to Lauze de Perret's house, he was just finishing his meal. But he immediately

received the messenger from Barbaroux in the
dining-room itself. There were half-a-dozen other
people at table. "I should like to speak to you
alone," she said, and they went into the drawing-
room. Lauze de Perret apologised. He had come
home late, and his friends had immediately claimed
his attention. So he had only just opened the parcel,
which he had put down on the mantelpiece, and
had not even had time to read the letter from Barbaroux.

When he had glanced at its contents, he asked
Charlotte for news of the refugees and placed himself at her disposal. She begged him to accompany
her to the Ministry of the Interior and help her to
get possession of Mademoiselle de Forbin's papers.
Although she was in a great hurry to settle the
business, she did not dare to ask him to go with
her at once; his friends were waiting for him.
"If you would be so kind as to come to my hotel
to-morrow morning," she said, "we could go to
see the Minister together."

He agreed, but pointed out with a smile that he
did not even know her name or where she was
staying. She handed him the hotel card, which she
had been given at the Messageries, and wrote her
name on it in pencil—Corday. As she was leaving
he invited her to have some refreshment, but she

refused. Returning to her room at about five o'clock, she fell asleep almost immediately.

.   .   .   .   .

On the following day, Friday, Lauze de Perret came to fetch her at about ten o'clock, and on their way he asked for details about Mademoiselle de Forbin's business and for news of the refugees in Caen. But when he tried to discuss politics, she became cautious and reserved, terrified of arousing suspicion. The name of Marat was not even mentioned.

At the Ministry of the Interior, an official informed them that the Minister received deputies only in the evening between eight and ten. So they parted, after having arranged to meet again in the evening.

To her great surprise, he returned in the afternoon. After he had left her, his house had been sealed and his correspondence seized. Suspicion against the Girondists was growing, and he was accused of being concerned with the Dillon conspiracy. "I am afraid," he said, "that I shall do you more harm than good by going with you to the Ministry. But in any case I have been thinking the matter over; you have no power of attorney from Mademoiselle de Forbin, and the officials will refuse to give you her papers."

Charlotte was obliged to agree that he was right, but she did not give up the idea of being of use to her friend. A few days later she was to give a touching proof of this. As Lauze de Perret was preparing to take his leave she held him back. She was so firmly convinced that she was going to restore peace to the world by ridding it of a monster that she had no fears for her involuntary allies and accomplices. Far from being seriously compromised, they too would be hailed as liberators. But Lauze de Perret was already compromised. The discovery that he had been in communication with her might, for a time at any rate, do harm to this obliging and courageous man. She wanted to avoid this if possible and to save him from all risk.

"Citizen du Perret," she said, "I have a little piece of advice to give you. Leave the Assembly and go away. You can easily do it. Go to Caen, where you and your colleagues can be of use to the commonwealth."

He answered sharply that his post was in Paris, and that nothing on earth would induce him to leave it. Anxious on his account and unable to give him any further explanation, she grew angry. "That's silly of you!" she exclaimed crossly.

Seeing that she was disappointed and upset, he good-naturedly promised her that he would let her know if he decided to go, and they would travel together. If not, he would give her a letter for Barbaroux. But he must know when she was going to leave Paris.

Determined not to compromise him further, she hastily answered that she did not know yet when she would be going back. And when he offered to come and get news on the following day, she immediately discouraged him and promised to write to him. No, no! He must on no account come back the next day! For that was to be Marat's last day on earth!

.   .   .   .   .

At seven o'clock on that Saturday morning, she was ready to go out. She was quietly dressed in brown. Into the opening of her bodice she slipped a piece of paper: "Address to those Frenchmen who are lovers of the law and of peace." She had written it on the previous evening after Lauze de Perret had gone. It was an ardent confession, in which she proclaimed aloud her faith and her sacrifice, her love of Peace and her hatred of hatred. They would find it on her warm with her life-blood, as it were part of herself on which her thought had been imprinted.

She described how she intended to put an end to the fratricidal struggle. "Already the indignant

departments are marching on Paris, already the fire
of civil war has spread over half this vast realm.
But there is still a means whereby it can be extin-
guished, though it must be done quickly ! "

She exonerated her deed in advance. She was
following the example of Hercules, who cleared the
world of monsters. " O France, thy peace depends
on the fulfilment of the Law. I am not assailing it
in killing Marat, who has been condemned by the
whole world. He is outside the Law. If I am guilty,
then Hercules too was guilty when he killed the
monsters. But did he ever meet one so odious ? "

And she passionately dedicated her life to her
love for humanity. " O my country, thy misfortunes
tear my heart. I can only offer thee my life, and I
thank Heaven for giving me the liberty to dispose
of it. No one will lose by my death ! I want my
last breath to be of use to my fellow-citizens, and
my head, when it is carried round Paris, to be a
rallying point for the friends of Law. May the
tottering Montagne see its downfall written in my
blood, and the world whose wrongs I have avenged
declare that I have deserved well at the hands of
men ! "

To this Address she pinned her baptismal certificate. For she would not be torn to pieces by the
mob from the galleries, as she had at first hoped.

She would not remain unrecognized in death as she had planned. She would be obliged to go to Marat's house and would no doubt have to give her name. She would be arrested and tried. In short, everybody would know who she was. So it would be better for them to learn from herself at once what she thought and who she was.

She reached the Palais Royal before eight o'clock. The shops were not yet open either in the Galeries de Bois or in the new arcades.[19] But she had to buy a weapon.

Ten times did she make the tour of the gardens. A newspaper boy was shouting the verdict in the Léonard Bourdon case. She bought a paper as she had been following the trial. Léonard Bourdon, the Montagnard deputy, was drunk one night when, as he was passing a guard-house of the Orleans regiment, he was challenged by the sentry. Instead of answering, he fired his pistol. There was a disturbance, and in the scuffle the deputy received a slight wound in the arm. To be avenged for what he called " his murder ", he had a state of siege declared and twenty-six persons arrested and brought up for trial. Nine of them had just been condemned to death. They were to be executed that very day. Charlotte burned with indignation. Another infamous outrage ! But it would be the last !

At length she found a cutler's shop open. A man, who was alone in the shop, sold her for two francs a freshly-ground kitchen knife, with a black handle in a shagreened sheath. She slipped it into her bodice.

It was still too early to call on Marat, and she sat down on a seat in the gardens which were gradually becoming animated. In spite of the fresh morning breeze, she was breathing heavily. She felt oppressed. A little child, playing about, came and fell against her knees, raising his beautiful innocent eyes to her face. She smiled at him and stroked his cheek. All her life she had been in the habit of making little presents for the pleasure of seeing a child's face light up with joy, from the time she had stuffed the village children with dainties in the bakehouse at Mesnil-Imbert to the moment when she gave her drawings to the little Lunel boy and bade him farewell for ever. But she had nothing to give this small Parisian. Yes, she had though! He would owe her a happier life. She was going to bring him Peace.

In the Place des Victoires she had noticed a cab rank. She got into one of the vehicles and told the driver to take her to Marat's house. He did not know the address; nor did she. She had not troubled to find out, so certain had she been of

H

killing him in the Convention. The driver made
enquiries among his comrades, and Charlotte wrote
down the address in pencil on a piece of paper:
"Faubourg St. Germain, Rue des Cordeliers, at the
top of the street."

It was about eleven o'clock when the cab drew
up at 30 Rue des Cordeliers, in front of a tall
grey house. Charlotte entered the porch and
stopped at the caretaker's lodge, where two women
of about thirty years of age were gossiping
together. She asked for Citizen Marat's flat.
"First floor front," the porter's wife answered absent‹
mindedly.

In the courtyard, on the right, Charlotte found,
under an arcade, a staircase with a wrought‹iron
balustrade. She ran quickly up it and rang the bell.
In the open doorway there appeared two young
women who were very much alike. Charlotte soon
learnt that she had before her Marat's companion,
Simonne Evrard,[20] and her younger sister, Catherine
Evrard. She asked to be allowed to have a word
with Citizen Marat. She had come from Caen. She
had some extremely interesting and urgent news to
give him. But the two women refused to tell Marat
that she was there. He was ill. He could not see
anybody.

Charlotte urged that she had important secrets

which it was imperative for him to know. Under her calm exterior she was bursting with impatience. She must obey her own commands. She must kill the monster. To think that he was there, quite close, perhaps behind that partition! But his two guardians were adamant. The elder more particularly refused to listen to anything she had to say and told her she would never be able to see him. And when Charlotte begged her at least to let her know when she could come back, this woman told her without beating about the bush that any further attempt on her part would be utterly useless, as it was impossible to say when Marat would be well again.

She was obliged to go away. But she was determined to return. By hook or by crook, she would force an entry. Since she was obliged to do so, she would have recourse to guile. Had not her " oracle " Raynal, written: " Tyrants do not deserve to be told the truth " ? To tempt Marat, she would write him a letter saying she could give him information about the insurrection in Normandy. He was bound to be taken in by the offer. Had he not for years been denouncing one great plot a day? She would even go to the length of flattering the patriotic pretentions of this " good Frenchman " who was not even French !

On returning to her room, she wrote:

" I have come from Caen. Your love for your country must make you wish to know about the conspiracies that are being hatched there. I await your reply."

She made enquiries in the office of her hotel, and discovered that letters were promptly delivered by the *petite poste*. Marat ought to receive the one she had written at about seven o'clock. So she would go to his house at about half-past seven.

She even took precautions in case the first letter did not reach him, and wrote another which she would take herself to the Rue des Cordeliers, and if necessary send it in to him. And again she lied and flattered his vanity, pretending this time to believe in his good sense and kindness of heart.

" I wrote to you this morning, Marat. Have you received my letter ? May I hope to see you for a moment ? If you have received it, I hope you will not refuse me, because what I have to tell you is extremely interesting. Surely it is enough that I am very miserable for me to have a right to your protection ! "

The wait in her stuffy room at the hotel seemed endless. She was suffocating. But she did not want to go out. There was nothing to tempt her to do so. Her object alone attracted her. What was the good of collecting souvenirs? In three days they would no doubt have disappeared with herself.

Detached though she was from the world, she nevertheless took the greatest pains with her dress.[21] Once again, as at all great moments of her life, her vanity was aroused. In the morning she had certainly been too quietly dressed. She must make a good impression on those women who were guarding Marat. She put on a gown of spotted *bazin* over a grey underskirt, covering her shoulders with a pale pink scarf, as the bodice was cut a little low in the neck. In her neatly gloved hand she held a fan. On her head she wore a tall hat with a black cockade and green ribbons. The high heeled shoes which she had ordered especially for her journey made her even taller.

Seven o'clock! Once again she took a cab to the Rue des Cordeliers. She told it to wait. She might want it if she was again refused admittance, or if, by some miracle, she was able to escape after she had killed Marat.

The porter's lodge was empty when she passed it, and climbing the wrought-iron staircase, she rang the bell. The porter's wife, who was no

doubt employed by Marat, opened the door to
her. But she too barred the way. Citizen Marat
could not see anybody. Besides, he was in his bath.
And to show that the interview was at an end, she
returned to her work, helping a commissionaire to
fold up newspapers in the hall.

Urged on by an invisible force, Charlotte became
exasperated by the difficulties she was encountering.
She almost screamed as she told the woman that she
had already called in the morning²² and had come
a very long way on purpose to see Marat. Moreover,
she had written to him by the *petite poste*, and
wanted to know whether he had received her letter.
The woman still continued folding up the news/
papers, and replied in a voice quite as loud that
Citizen Marat received a great many letters and she
couldn't say whether he had received Charlotte's
or not.

At this juncture Simonne Evrard appeared. Marat
had heard the altercation. He had just received the
letter Charlotte had posted, and had given instruc/
tions for her to be shown in. At last !

The young woman led the way through two small
rooms and left her in the bathroom. It was a narrow
almost dark closet, and the evening light filtered in
through a window with greenish panes. The hot
damp air smelt like a swamp, and Charlotte felt as

though she were under water. On the left she at
last saw Marat in a slipper bath made of copper.

He was wearing a dressing-gown and had a wet
towel round his head. A board laid across the bath
was covered with papers and newspapers, and at his
side was an inkstand on a wooden block.

He pointed to the only chair, which was standing
with its back to the window, and going straight to
the point, asked for information about the insurrection in Normandy, enquiring the names of the
Girondists who had taken refuge in Caen and
writing them down to her dictation.

At last she saw the face that had been haunting
her for ten months ! Age and illness had made it
even more horrible—the leaden complexion, the
round yellow eyes, and the nose squashed down over
the toad-like mouth. Every time he moved she
could see on his neck and shoulders the leprosy that
was eating away his body. He was indeed a monster !
He was *the* monster !

But Simonne Evrard glided into the room. Had
she been moved by some presentiment ? Had she
made some excuse to come in ? She consulted
Marat about a mixture of loam and almond water
which he used to drink as medicine.

For the first time Charlotte looked round the
room, and instinctively took in the details; there

were paintings on the pale coloured paper of shafts of columns, a map of the French departments, and two pistols crossed under an inscription in large letters: DEATH! What irony!

Simonne Evrard went out, taking with her two dishes that had been placed on the window-sill for the evening meal. Perhaps she was afraid of poison.

Marat continued his cross-questioning, and wrote down the names of the Calvados officials who had been sent as delegates to Évreux. She gave the name of Bougon-Longrais and the others. What matter if she seemed to be betraying them? She was going to save them.

He stopped writing. "I shall have them guillo- tined in Paris in a day or two," he sniggered.

These words decided his fate. With one swift movement she sprang to her feet, drew the knife from her bosom and brought it down with a terrific force of which she did not know she was capable! And she immediately felt an indescribable sense of relief.

Marat gave only one hoarse incoherent cry. Charlotte rushed through the two rooms separating her from the hall. She was going to escape. No! The commissionaire, who was folding up the news- papers, had heard Marat's cry and when he saw the girl he understood. "Help! Help! Murder!"

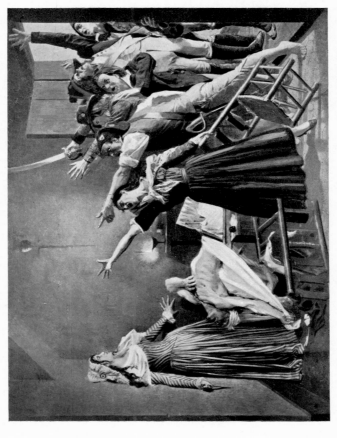

THE ASSASSINATION OF MARAT BY CHARLOTTE CORDAY

From a painting by J. J. Wiertz

he yelled. And brandishing a chair he brought it down on her. The women rushed in, and throwing themselves on her brought her to the floor. As she tried to get up, the man seized her roughly by the breast and again flung her down, raining blows and curses upon her: " You jade ! You wretch ! "

A surgeon, who lived in the house, hurried in, leapt over the struggling figures and disappeared in the direction of the bathroom. Armed men seized Charlotte, raised her from the floor, bound her hands tightly behind her back, and mounted guard over her in a corner of the hall. Suddenly, above the din and shouting of orders, the cries of rage and the lamentations that filled the place, she heard the words: " He is dead ! "

Thus she learnt that she had dealt a mortal blow, and that Marat was no more ! Little did she care now for the bruises that were making her cheeks burn, her torn clothes, the cords that cut into her wrists and the fate that awaited her. Peace had been restored !

A police officer, followed by his acolytes, proceeded to take evidence. In a little while he had Charlotte brought into the drawing-room. It was lighted by lamps and gay with flowers. Under the windows looking out on to the street the dull roar of the mob could be heard. The examination began, rigorous and minute. Charlotte had to give details of her life, her journey, how she had spent her time in Paris, the murder, and the reasons that had led her to commit it. The man was anxious to find accomplices at all costs. But she had recovered her composure and denied having been guided or advised by anybody. She even had the presence of mind during this first assault upon her not to men*tion the interviews she had had with Lauze de Perret.

Four men pushed their way into the drawing*room. They were members of the Convention, sent by the Committee of Public Safety. They gave their names to the police officer. From prints and caricatures Charlotte recognised them as Legendre, Chabot, Drouet. . . .

It was in the presence of these newcomers that the police officer ordered Charlotte to be searched. This was an unexpected ordeal. She imagined she had thought of everything ! Who knows ? If she had guessed what was going to happen she might perhaps have given up her plan. Her outraged modesty made her suffer tortures when she felt the hands of the police and the eyes of the other men upon her.

They took from her pocket her money, her thimble and her ball of cotton. Her pocket*book contained her passport and the second letter she had prepared for Marat. In her bodice they found the sheath of the knife and her baptismal certificate pinned to the "Address to Frenchmen."

Chabot maintained that he could see another paper in the opening, and stretched out his hand. As she was sitting down with her hands tied behind her back, Charlotte was unable to defend herself. She instinctively drew back, but the movement made her bodice fly wide open. Filled with confusion and despair she begged to be allowed to tidy herself, and without waiting for permission, she hid her bosom as best she could by bending forward till her chin touched her knees. The men had pity on her and allowed her hands to be untied. She raised herself and turning to the wall quickly readjusted her clothes.

As soon as she had done so, she recovered her composure. And when they read over the evidence to her before giving it to her to sign she corrected her answers in seven places as they had been inaccurately taken down. When the police wished to tie her hands behind her back again, she calmly asked to be allowed to pull down her sleeves and put on her gloves, "if they would be so good as to save her suffering before putting her to death."

She held her own against the members of the Convention who, as soon as the evidence had been signed, continued to harass her with questions. Legendre maintained that she had called at his house in the morning. " You are wrong, Citizen," she retorted. " I never gave you a thought! I don't think you have the capacity to be tyrant of your country. I had no intention of punishing so many people."

" Who taught you how to pierce Marat to the heart at the first blow? " demanded Chabot.

" The indignation that filled my own! " she replied.

When Chabot proceeded to tell her that he intended to keep her watch, she remembered that he belonged to the Church. " Have you forgotten that the Capucins have taken the vow of poverty? " she replied scathingly.

But a further trial awaited her—the confrontation with her victim. She was taken to the brilliantly lighted room in which it had already become necessary to burn aromatics, and made to face the mask, hideously contracted in death and looking even more repulsive than it had done in life. They uncovered the gaping wound on the right side of his chest which was eaten away with leprosy. But she was upset most of all by the sobs of the woman bending over the foot of the bed—Simonne Evrard, Marat's companion, of whose very existence she had been ignorant in the morning. She felt no regret for her crime, but the woman's grief was intolerable to her. " Yes, yes," she exclaimed irritably, impatient to be gone, " I killed him ! "

It was midnight when Drouet and Chabot took her to the Abbaye prison.[23] The great gate was opened to let her in and from the pitch black street, which the crowds seemed to make even darker, rose a loud ferocious cry for her blood. Her guards, pushing away the maddened mob, hurled her back into the cab, which was still waiting. But the howling crowd surrounded it and prevented it from moving. Charlotte too was to pay the penalty of her life. What matter ? She had accomplished her task ! Meanwhile Drouet, raising his voice, called upon the people, in the name of the Law, to be quiet and go away without making a disturbance. They obeyed. During the interval Charlotte had fainted.

CHAPTER VII

THE JUDGES

IN THE Abbaye prison which was connected with the old monastery of St. Germain des Prés, Charlotte was put in the cell lately occupied by the Girondist Brissot. She learnt this from the concierge, Lavacquerie, who immediately showed her the utmost kindness and consideration.

She did not know that Brissot himself had succeeded Madame Roland, who in her Memoirs describes her cramped lugubrious quarters, with their dirty grey walls and stout bars. Moreover, the cell was quite close to a wood shed infested with all the animals of the prison and which smelt abominably. But in spite of this it was much sought after, for it was too small to hold two beds and there was a possibility of the prisoner having it all to himself.

But Charlotte was not allowed this privilege. The gendarmes kept constant watch over her. During the night she found their presence extremely disagreeable, and she wrote complaining to the Committee of Public Safety, but without avail.

During her first day in prison, Sunday, the 14th of July, she immediately set to work to mend her dress which had been torn when she was arrested. She had no change of clothes as, after the Hôtel de la Providence had been searched the previous evening, all her belongings had been seized.[24]

In spite of the fact that she had nothing, her vanity was again aroused. She wanted to appear before the revolutionary Tribunal in a Normandy cap. She thought it suited her better than her hat with the cockade which, moreover, had been battered in the scuffle. She resolved to make a new headress for herself. She was an expert at the job, and the two Lavacqueries furnished her with all the materials she required.

.   .   .   .   .   .

On Monday, the 15th, she kept her promise to write to tell Barbaroux[25] all about her journey. But though her letter was addressed to him, the Girondist, she meant it for all her relatives and friends and anybody who took an interest in her. Its seven sheets, in which there was not a single erasure, written in the interval between the murder and the scaffold, illumined alternately by her burning love and her roguish grace, bear eloquent testimony to her astounding freedom of thought.

In them the whole drama is reflected and concentrated.

She began with the brief and charming description of her journey in which she made fun of the
love-lorn swain " who doubtless liked women when
they were asleep." She went on to explain how the
review of the 7th of July had determined the date of
her departure, and described her original plan. " At
that time my idea was to remain unknown, to kill
Marat publicly and be killed myself at once, leaving
the people of Paris to make a vain search to discover
who I was."

She told him how, when she arrived in Paris, she
was afraid of compromising Lauze de Perret, and
tried to save him by telling him to go to Caen.
She confessed that she was obliged to have recourse
to a " shameful artifice " to gain access to Marat.
But she invoked " my oracle, Raynal," who had said
that tyrants did not deserve to be told the truth.

About the murder itself she said very little.
" The newspapers will tell you all about that," she
wrote. But she quoted Marat's last words which
had decided his fate. They ought to be written in
letters of gold on his statue, she added ironically.
For her hatred of Marat was as strong as ever. It
burst out on every page. " I have hated only one
person in my life, and I have proved the strength of

my hatred. . . . He was a ravening monster who would have devoured the whole of France. . . . Thank God he was not a Frenchman born ! "

Then came the examination in Marat's drawing-room—Chabot, cynical " looking like a madman ", Legendre pompous, and the police officer determined to discover accomplices. They were not satisfied with " having only an insignificant woman to offer to the shade of the great man."

On setting out for the prison, she thought she would be killed. She was ready for it. " I was expecting to die at any moment." But some brave men saved her from the " excusable fury " of the mob.

In the prison itself she declared that she was treated with " the utmost consideration ",[26] and that the concierges were " the best and kindest of souls." She ingenuously confessed that " she whiled away the time writing songs." That is to say, she copied out for the other prisoners the couplets broadcast by the Girondists at Caen which constituted an important method of propaganda. But she complained of the constant presence of the two gendarmes. They had been provided " to prevent me from being bored; that was all right during the day, but at night it is extremely disagreeable. . . . I think it was Chabot's idea; only a Capuchin could have thought of such a thing."

I

Lastly, after begging Barbaroux to forgive her if some jokes at his expense came to light in her letters to her father, she placed her relatives and friends under the protection of the Girondists.

For she was certain that they would return to Paris in power. Had she not restored Peace to the country ? Peace ! Of that at least she was certain. The whole of her letter bears witness to this, including the address at the head: " From the Abbaye Prison, in the cell vacated by Brissot, on the second day of the preparations for peace." In her eyes Peace was inaugurated by the death of Marat. That was the grand preliminary; without it they would never have had Peace ! In ten places she hails the restoration of Peace. " May Peace be established as quickly as I hope it will. . . . The foundations of Peace must be laid." And overjoyed at the release of her country, she addresses the following words to it: " I have been revelling in Peace for the last two days; my country's good is my own."

.   .   .   .   .

On the evening of that same Monday she made a further request to the Committee of Public Safety. She asked to have a miniature of herself painted to be handed over to her family and political friends. And still outraged in her modesty she again begged " to be allowed to sleep alone." The letter ran as follows :

" To the Citizens composing the Committee of Public Safety,

" As I still have a few hours to live, may I be allowed to hope, Citizens, that you will allow me to have my portrait painted ? I should like to leave it as a memento to my friends. Moreover, just as the likenesses of good citizens are cherished and held in honour, so curiosity may sometimes lead to a desire to know what great criminals looked like, since this would serve to perpetuate the horror felt for their crimes. If you deign to heed my request, I beg you to send me a miniature painter to-morrow. I take this opportunity of repeating the request to be allowed to sleep alone. Assuring you of my deepest gratitude,

" MARIE CORDAY.

" I am constantly hearing it being shouted in the streets that Fauchet has been arrested for being my accomplice. But I have never set eyes upon him, except through the window, and that was more than two years ago. I neither like nor respect him. I have always regarded him as a fanatic entirely lacking in determination. He was the last man in the world to whom I would have cared to entrust a secret. If this declaration can be of any use to him, I swear to its truth."

Even in this short letter her irony and her kind‹
ness of heart are displayed. It is in irony that she
compares herself to the great criminals whose por‹
traits and misdeeds are calculated to inspire horror
for evermore, for she was convinced that she had
delivered her country from a monster. And it was
out of kindness of heart that, in the name of justice,
she tried to save Fauchet, a man whom she despised.

.   .   .   .   .

On the morning of the 16th she appeared before
Montané, the President of the Revolutionary Tri‹
bunal. Her examination, although it was long and
detailed, was very similar to the one she had under‹
gone at the hands of the police officer on the evening
of the murder. Both men were equally obsessed
by the desire to find accomplices.

Before dismissing her, Montané asked whether
she had anyone to defend her. She chose her friend,
Gustave Doulcet, who was now a member of the
Convention. The public prosecutor, Fouquier‹Tin‹
ville, who was present at the examination, undertook
to inform him immediately.[27]

At the end of the day she was transferred to
the Conciergerie, which was at the entrance of the
Revolutionary Tribunal and, like it, situated in the
Palais de Justice. Here the charge preferred against

her by Fouquier-Tinville was read over to her, as well as a list of witnesses and the names of the jury.[28]

She was informed that she would be brought up for trial on the morning of the following day. "At midday, to use a Latin expression, I shall have lived," she wrote to Barbaroux. She was anxious to finish that evening the letter she had begun in the Abbaye Prison.

Her capacity for irony did not desert her on the eve of death. When she said she had chosen Gustave Doulcet to defend her, she added, "I thought of asking for Robespierre or Chabot."

But her tone was more serious than when she was writing from the Abbaye, and frequently she expressed herself as though she were making her last will and testament. She explains why she did not address this last letter to her friend Bougon-Langrais. She was not sure he was at Évreux and feared that his natural kindness of heart would make him feel overcome with grief at her death. "But I think he is a good enough citizen to find consolation in the hope of Peace. I know how much he longs for it, and I trust that in paving the way to it I have fulfilled his wishes."

Her certainty of having restored Peace is once more apparent in this letter. Thus she thought that

Lauze de Perret and Fauchet, who had been arrested on the previous day, would be immediately set free. And this conviction that she had served the cause of Peace upheld her continually. " I never had any regard for life except as a means of being useful." She did not fear death which was now so close at hand. But she did not know how her last moments would be spent. " It is the end that crowns the achievement."

On the eve of her death, among her last wishes, she recommended Mademoiselle de Forbin to the care of Barbaroux, and gave him her address in Switzerland: " I hope you will not cease to take an interest in Mme. Forbin's business . . . I beg you to tell her that I love her with all my heart."

She ends her farewells with the following words: " I commend myself to the memory of the true friends of Peace."

Lastly, that night she wrote to her father the following letter in which she exhales her whole soul, as it were with her last breath:

" Forgive me, my dear Father, for having disposed of my life without your permission. I have avenged many an innocent victim and prevented many a disaster. One day the people will learn the truth and rejoice in having been delivered from a tyrant. If I tried to make you believe that I was going to England, it was because I hoped to keep my identity unknown; but I found that impossible. I hope you will not be grieved. In any case, I think you will have friends in Caen. I have chosen Gustave Doulcet to defend me; but a crime like mine admits of no defence. I did so as a mere matter of form. Farewell, my dear Father; I beg you to forget me, or rather to rejoice in my fate. The cause for which I die is a noble one. I kiss my sister, whom I love with all my heart, as well as all my relatives. Do not forget Corneille's line:

" It is the crime that brings shame, and not the scaffold."

" To-morrow at eight o'clock I shall be brought up for trial. This 16th day of July."

.   .   .   .   .

On the next day, Wednesday, the 17th, at about eight o'clock in the morning, her guards conducted her from her cell through the Palais de Justice to the Tribunal. She was dressed as she had been on the evening when she forced her way into Marat's house, in her light spotted *bazin* dress. But on her head she wore her pleated lawn cap, from which her sunny locks escaped in ringlets over her shoulders.

She stopped in front of the concierge's lodge. The Richard couple, like the Lavacqueries at the

Abbaye, were extremely kind to her. She asked them to have her breakfast ready for her, as she expected to be back quite soon. "The gentlemen must be anxious to get the whole thing over," she said.

The audience chamber was full to overflowing. It was a long room, badly lighted by two windows high up in the wall. In spite of the early hour, it was uncomfortably hot. When Charlotte came in, a murmur of surprise rose from the crowded inquisi-tive benches. There was no booing. Her gentleness and youth and her calm proud modesty impressed even the fanatics who haunted the law courts and generally hooted the prisoners.

She took a seat. To her right, on a platform, sat the President and the three judges. They wore black suits and cloaks, white cravats, and plumed hats caught up on one side by a tricoloured cockade. Behind them the jury were arranged in a semi-circle. Straight in front of her, a man with a cruel and crafty face, was sitting alone at a table closely scrutinising her. She recognized him as the Public Prosecutor, the man who was going to demand her death, Fouquier-Tinville.

As soon as the questions concerning her identity had been settled, Montané, the President, asked whether she had anyone to defend her. Gustave

Doulcet had not replied. She was pained by his silence, and suspected him of trying to evade her request. "I had chosen a friend," she replied in her musical, almost childish voice, "but I have heard nothing of him since yesterday. Apparently, he has not had the courage to undertake my defence."

The President, seeing the lawyer Chauveau-Lagarde in the hall, called upon him to undertake the task.

Charlotte listened absent-mindedly to the indictment. What was the good of all these formalities? She confessed everything. She knew her fate. She was even more anxious than the judges to get the whole matter over and done with.

The witnesses filed past. She learnt the names of most of them. Feuillard, the waiter at the Hôtel de la Providence; Laurent Bas, the commissionaire who had knocked her down and brutally seized her by the breast. Madame Pain, the porter's wife, who had tried to refuse her admittance to the hall in the evening. Jeannette Maréchal, the cook, who had been gossiping in the lodge with the woman in the morning. Lafondée, the surgeon-dentist, who had been the first to declare that Marat was dead.

After the evidence of each witness had been taken, she confirmed it, merely saying, "It is perfectly true." Once she added, "I have nothing to say, except that I succeeded." She would have liked to hurry over the evidence and have done with it.

She even interrupted Simonne Evrard's account of the matter. The woman's tears upset her as they had done on the night when she had been confronted with the body. "Yes, yes," she said hurriedly, "I killed him." But she displayed no further emotion until she was shown the knife, when she turned away waving it aside. "Yes, I recognize it, I recognize it," she exclaimed with the same hasty impatience.

But some of the witnesses were mistaken. A certain Joseph Hénoque, employed at the Mairie, swore that he had received Charlotte Corday in his office on the evening of Friday the 12th. She replied that she did not even know where the Mairie was.

A woman named Lebourgeois, who kept a wineshop, insisted that she had seen Charlotte in one of the galleries at the Convention on Thursday, the 11th, in the company of Lauze de Perret and Fauchet. She even declared she recognized these two men, who had been arrested the previous day and brought from prison to appear as witnesses. Naturally, they protested violently.

During the course of these investigations, the President cross-examined Charlotte about the crime.

She again pointed out that she had made up her mind after the affair of the 31st of May, and that her original intention had been to kill Marat on the summit of the Montagne. "If I had thought I could have succeeded in that way, I should have preferred it to any other method. For I knew that in that case I should inevitably fall a victim to the fury of the mob. And that is what I wanted. People thought I was in London. Nobody would have known my name."

But later on she had been obliged to change her plans and kill Marat in his own house. And she agreed that she would have crossed over to England if she had not been arrested.

Twice Montané reproached her with having used hypocritical subterfuges in order to obtain access to Marat. She confessed that such methods were unworthy of her, but added that "they were all justified for the salvation of her country."

Montané was guilty of some confusion[29] in thinking that Marat had received the letter in which she begged for his protection and which she had kept on her, since she had succeeded in trapping him by promising to reveal the Norman conspiracy. "How could you have regarded Marat as a monster," he enquired, "when he allowed you to obtain access to him purely owing to his humanity because you had written to tell him you were persecuted?"

"What did his humanity to me matter, if he had proved a monster to other people?" she replied simply, not grasping the fundamental mistake the President had made.

The altercation between her and Montané grew heated and acrimonious only when he obstinately persisted in trying to discover accomplices.

"But who inspired you with such hatred for Marat?"

"I did not require any hatred on the part of other people. I hated him enough myself."

"But the idea of killing him must have been suggested to you by somebody! Who urged you to commit this murder?"

"One does a thing badly if one has not thought it all out oneself!"

"What was it you hated in him?"

"His crimes!"

"What do you mean by his crimes?"

"The devastation of France."

"What did you hope to achieve by killing him?"

"The restoration of Peace to my country."

"Do you imagine that you have killed all the Marats then?"

"He is dead, and perhaps the others will be frightened."

Again and again he returned to the charge.

"How do you expect anybody to believe that you were not influenced by anybody when you say that you regarded Marat as having been responsible for all the ills that have befallen France, though he was constantly unmasking traitors and conspirators?"

"It is only in Paris that people are hypnotized by Marat. In the provinces he is regarded as a monster."

Montané shrewdly suspected that it was the refugees who had prompted her to her crime. But she denied this so vehemently that he was obliged to seek elsewhere.

"Then it must have been the newspapers you read that informed you that Marat was an anarchist?"

"Yes," she replied in memorable words. "I knew that he was corrupting France. I killed one man in order to save thousands. I was a Republican long before the Revolution!"

The President was obliged to abandon his efforts to discover accomplices. Moreover, it seemed at times as though he too were unbending and, like the crowd, the jury and even the judges, succumbing to the limpid charm of her voice and everything about her.

Nevertheless, he insisted in cold convincing tones that she must have practised beforehand to have succeeded in dealing Marat a mortal blow. According to the medical reports, she would not have killed him if she had struck in any other way.

"I struck anyhow," she replied. "It was mere chance."

Fouquier-Tinville had not troubled to exert himself much, so convinced was he of obtaining his prey. But he emphasized this incident. She had struck from above downwards in such a way as to make sure of her victim. "You must have practised a great deal for this crime," he insisted.

But she was so convinced of having delivered the world of a scourge that she was thunderstruck:

"Oh! The monster! He takes me for a murderess!" she exclaimed indignantly.

The cross-examination was over. But Charlotte still had to listen to the reading of the letters she had written in prison. Her face, reflecting her thoughts, darkened as she heard her farewell to her father, and lit up with pride at the quotation from Thomas Corneille : "It is the crime that brings shame, and not the scaffold." And she could not refrain from smiling at the passage in her letter to Barbaroux: "I think it was Chabot's idea; only a Capuchin could have thought of such a thing."

She relied on the Tribunal to see that these letters reached the persons to whom they were addressed. The President, without making any promise, asked her whether she had anything to add to them.

" I have left out one sentence from the letter to Barbaroux," she replied. " I should like to add: ' The anarchist leader is no more. You will have Peace ! ' "

Fouquier,Tinville rose from his seat. A lengthy speech for the prosecution was utterly unnecessary. And quite briefly he demanded the prisoner's head.

The President gave the floor to the counsel for the defence. During the cross,examination the jury had sent a message to Chauveau,Lagarde, telling him not to speak, and Montané had undertaken to put forward a plea of insanity on behalf of the prisoner. Charlotte guessed what was going on. She was afraid he would do as he was told, or else attempt to belittle her great act by giving petty reasons for it. But she heard him putting the whole blame for the crime down to the smallest detail on to her. As though he had understood what she wanted, he confined himself to making a brief plea of political passion in her defence.

" That imperturbable calm and that entire abne, gation of self which show no sign of remorse, so to speak, even in the very presence of death itself, that calm and that abnegation, in their way sublime, are not natural. They can be explained only on the basis of the exaltation due to the political fanaticism which put the dagger into her hand. And it is for you, Citizens of the Jury, to judge how much weight to assign, in the scales of justice, to this moral consideration. I rely on your discretion.''

From that moment she ceased to take any interest in the formalities of the trial—the President's summing up, the short deliberation on the part of the jury, their unanimous reply to the three questions put to them, and the concluding remarks of Fouquier-Tinville. She was anxious to escape from the stifling hall. When Montané asked her whether she had anything to say why the law should not be carried out she did not even reply. And when the judges returned their verdict in loud tones and the President pronounced sentence of death, she remained so calm and collected that she seemed not to have heard.

It was midday. "To the Public Prosecutor's coach!" The execution was to take place the same day, in the Place de la Révolution, at five o'clock.

CHAPTER VIII

THE LAST HOURS

AS SOON as sentence had been passed, Charlotte turned to Chauveau-Lagarde, and thanked him for having defended her " in a manner worthy of himself and of her." She wanted to give him a proof of confidence and to appeal to him as to her last friend on earth. As soon as the Tribunal had made known the verdict, her belongings were confiscated. She had left a trifling debt behind her in the prison, a matter of thirty francs in *assignats*. She begged Chauveau-Lagarde to pay it for her. " I rely on your generosity," she said.

On the way to her cell, she met the concierge Richard and his wife. They were still keeping her breakfast for her. " The judges detained me such a long time up there," she said with a smile, " that you must excuse me for breaking my word."

At this moment a priest came up to her, the Abbé Lothringer, one of the three ecclesiastics charged with the task of ministering to the spiritual wants of prisoners condemned to death. He offered her his services. During the course of the trial, Charlotte had had an opportunity of making her religious views known. When President Montané asked her whether she usually confessed to a priest who had taken the oath or to a refractory priest, she answered that she did not go to either, and that she had no confessor. She therefore gently refused the Abbé's offer. " Please thank those who were good enough to send you," she said. " I am extremely grateful to them, but I do not require your ministrations."

As soon as she entered her cell, Richard, the concierge, came in and told her that an artist had come to paint her portrait. She was expecting him. She had noticed him at the trial when he had made a rough sketch on his canvas. And she was pleased to think that the Committee of Public Safety had granted her request, though somewhat late in the day. As soon as the trial was over, she had openly asked that he might be allowed to finish his work in her cell.

The artist presented himself to her. His name was Jean Jacques Hauer.[30] He had met with no difficulty in obtaining permission to enter the prison, for he was an officer in the National Guard, and a well-known figure in his own section.

She graciously thanked him and sat down on a chair. " I am ready," she said. She talked calmly and cheerfully to him with the easy manner of a woman of the world, and referred to the act she had committed. Far from regretting it, she again congratulated herself on having delivered France from a monster. Now and again she would rise and examine the portrait congratulating the artist, and suggesting some slight alteration.

Meanwhile, time was flying. She wanted to send off another letter, and to avoid interrupting the artist at his work, she placed a book under her hand as a rest and began to write without leaving her chair.

At this moment Richard opened the door and hid himself behind a group of men. One of them was carrying on his arms the red smock worn by murderers for their execution. She understood. It was Sanson, the executioner ! She could not control her agitation. " What ? Already ! " But she quickly recovered her self-possession, and asked the man for permission to finish her letter.

" Citizen Doulcet de Pontécoulant is a coward for refusing to defend me when the task was so easy. The man who undertook it carried it out with the utmost possible dignity. I shall be grateful to him for it till my last moment.

" MARIE DE CORDAY."

This last moment had arrived. She folded up the piece of paper in the shape of a letter, while one of the two ushers who had accompanied the executioner read out her sentence to her. She begged him to see that her note reached the man to whom it was addressed, the deputy Gustave Doulcet.

Sanson was holding a pair of scissors in his hand. She sat down, took off her cap, unloosed her beautiful hair, and signed to the executioner to cut it off. When it had fallen to the floor she picked up a lock of it and handed it to the artist Hauer: "I thank you for what you have done for me, sir. All I can offer you as a sign of my gratitude is this souvenir from a dying woman." She then asked Richard to give the rest to his wife.

She put on the red smock herself. It was cut very low, and she obtained permission to put her pink scarf round her shoulders. As they were going to tie her hands behind her back, she asked to be allowed to put on her gloves. Her guards had drawn the cords so tight at Marat's house that she still had the marks on her wrists. But Sanson assured her that he would bind her without hurting her. "That's true," she observed with a smile; "the others were not so accustomed to it as you are."

Thus the last touches were put to the rough and ready toilet of death, "which," as she said, "leads to immortality." It was past six o'clock. The cart was waiting in the court. Charlotte wanted to remain standing, leaning against the side. But Sanson had placed a stool beside her on which she could rest her knee.

The crowd was surging round the Palais. In addition to those who always made a point of witnessing executions and the usual rabid mob, there were the innumerable fanatical adherents of Marat. At sight of the prisoner, a loud roar for her death rose from the multitude, and shaking fists, infuriated faces, and wide open mouths surrounded the cart.

Just at this moment a storm which had been brewing ever since the morning burst out in full fury. But the rain did not disperse the crowd, whose shouts drowned the growl of the thunder.

Charlotte met the hooting and howling with her characteristic smile and proud, calm bearing. " I am giving them Peace ! " she said to herself, as they howled for her death and shook their fists at her. This was the secret of her serenity. With her hands tied behind her back, she remained standing with her head held high. No, her old friends could not have taken her to task that day for " hiding her beautiful eyes." Her red smock, drenched with rain, clung to her body like the draperies on a statue.

It seemed as though her resolute gentleness and limpid grace again enjoined silence and respect. As the storm died down the curses and imprecations also grew few and far between, although the crowd along the quays and in the streets was still as dense. Only the most rabid fanatics followed the cart, kept at a distance by the mounted guards, and persistently vomited forth their dastardly insults.

In the Rue St Honoré the cart made its way more slowly than ever. "It's a long way, isn't it?" observed Sanson, moved by a courage he had never before witnessed. "Bah! We are certain of getting there!" she smilingly replied in her musical, almost childish voice.

It was nearly eight o'clock when the Place de la Révolution came in sight. The fiery rays of the setting sun lit up the horizon. The executioner wanted to hide the sight of the guillotine from his young victim. But she leant forward eagerly. "I have a right to be curious," she observed. "I have never seen one before."

In spite of her fetters, she lightly scaled the slippery steps of the scaffold without requiring help. When one of the assistants took off her scarf and uncovered her shoulders she turned pale and started back violently. It was the last supreme revolt of her outraged modesty. She feared men's eyes on her neck much more than she feared the guillotine. But once again for the last time she recovered her composure. The bright fresh colour returned to her cheeks and she looked as though she were inspired. She threw herself of her own accord on to the block and the falling of the knife was the only sound to break the profound silence that reigned all round.

One or two cries of " Vive la Nation ! Vive la République ! " rose from the crowd which, surging forward in one unbroken stream, had flooded the huge square. An assistant carpenter, who had adjusted the guillotine, seized the head by the hair to show it to the people. It seemed to be smiling still. And he gave it two slaps on the cheeks.

CHAPTER IX

AFTERWARDS . . .

THAT outrageous act gave rise to a murmur of horror and indignation from the crowd. Disowned by Sanson, who had employed him only as a temporary assistant, Legros, who was a low lout, was condemned by the police court to a week's imprisonment, to public censure and to exposure for six hours on the Place de la Révolution, where he had committed the outrage. Roussillon, one of the members of the Revolutionary Tribunal, lodged a protest against the man in an open letter. After describing the punishment inflicted upon him, he added: " I felt it my duty to make known this act of justice to the public who, ever great and ever just, will approve what the Friend of the People himself would have approved had he recovered from his wound. He was too great ever to have sanctioned such baseness. He knew, and all the world ought to know, that when the crime has been punished the law is satisfied ! "

At this dastardly insult, it is said that Charlotte

Corday's face blushed. The legend gave rise to hot controversies. Among her contemporaries, scientific men, like Cabanis, refused to believe in the genuineness of the phenomenon. Others, like Doctor Sue, the father of the novelist, Eugène Sue, and the naturalist Soemmering, maintained that it was a proof of survival after death. While yet others, like Doctor Léveillé, declared that the brutal blow had caused a perfectly mechanical congestion. Another explanation was that the blush was merely the mark left by the lout's bloodstained hand. Long afterwards, Michelet suggested that the fiery rays of the setting sun had cast a crimson reflection on the sweet face of the dead girl.

From the Place de la Révolution the remains of Charlotte Corday[31] were conveyed to the Hôpital de la Charité, where they were examined by two doctors in the presence of two members of the Convention, one of whom was David the artist. Since Marat's death, the most venomous calumnies had been circulated about the dead girl. More particularly she was accused of having been merely the instrument of Barbaroux, whom she had obeyed from love, after she had given herself to him. Apparently, the men who examined her tried after her death to find evidence of her lapse from virtue. But they were forced to acknowledge her virgin purity.[32]

She was buried in the Madeleine Cemetery, in the Rue d'Anjou St Honoré, almost on the site of the present Chapelle Expiatoire. In 1815 the bones from the Madeleine were taken away and buried in a common burial ground in the Plaine des Mousseaux, now the Plaine Monceau.

.   .   .   .   .

What became of Charlotte's relatives and friends after her death ?

Her friend Bougon-Longrais was at Évreux when she set out for Paris but he was suddenly recalled to Caen. And indeed events moved quickly. On the 13th of July, the very day of Marat's death, the volunteers, under General de Wimpffen, met the forces sent by the Montagne from Paris between Cocherel and Brécourt. There was a skirmish and ten cannon shots were exchanged. Both parties fell back thinking they had been defeated. But the Paris troops, which were called the Army of Peace, recovered first, and failing to meet any enemy, advanced victoriously on Lisieux and then on Caen. This was the end of the insurrection in Normandy.

The majority of those who had been compromised in the movement were outlawed. Bougon-Longrais was obliged to take flight. He was hunted down

from village to village. At Longueval he was almost
caught in his hiding-place. In a garment which he
was obliged to leave behind him, the gendarmes
discovered his will, and in it a lock of hair.

Later on, he fell into the hands of the Vendéens.
The Prince de Talmond took a fancy to him and
made him his secretary. But they were both arrested
near Fougères. After a brief trial, Bougon-Longrais
was executed at Rennes on the 5th of January, 1794.
At eight o'clock in the morning, before he set out
to meet his doom, he wrote a long letter to his
mother in which he again invoked the name of
Charlotte.

" If only, like my beloved Charlotte, I had been
able in my last moments to lull myself to sleep with
a sweet and deceptive illusion, and believe that peace
and order would soon be restored to my country !
But I cannot ! I am leaving this world tormented
by the idea that blood is going to flow in ever
greater torrents ! Oh Charlotte Corday ! Oh my
noble and generous friend ! The memory of you
has never ceased to fill my mind and my heart.
Wait for me, I am coming to you ! The desire to
avenge you has made me bear with life until this
moment. But I think I have now satisfied the
demands of this sacred duty. I die happy and
worthy of you."

As for Gustave Doulcet, the accusation brought against him by Charlotte in the note she addressed to him just before she died was unjust. When he received it, already opened, on the 20th of July, he was horrified. He had no idea that Charlotte had asked to have him to defend her. He wrote demanding an explanation from Montané, who immediately gave it. On the 16th of July the Public Prosecutor had, as a matter of fact, informed Gustave Doulcet that the prisoner had chosen him as her counsel. But the gendarme entrusted with the duty of delivering Fouquier-Tinville's letter had failed to find the man to whom it was addressed, and had returned it too late to the Public Prosecutor.

Gustave Doulcet was not surprised that the gendarme had not been able to find him. Knowing that he was suspect, he used to change his abode every evening. But Charlotte's unfounded reproach was intolerable and he addressed a protest to all the newspapers: " It was four days after her execution that the Revolutionary Tribunal informed me of the choice made by Marie Corday."

Throughout his long life, he maintained that he regretted his ignorance of Mademoiselle de Corday's choice and that he would have accepted the " dangerous honour of defending her, because they were

united by ties of blood and by political views shared
in common."

President of the Convention in 1795, of the
Council of Five Hundred in 1796, Count and
Senator of the Empire and a peer of France under
the Restoration, he died in 1853 at the age of nearly
ninety.

Mademoiselle de Faudoas, one of Charlotte Cor⁄
day's friends, perished a year after Charlotte's
execution. Her father, the Marquis de Faudoas,
a staunch Royalist, had remained one of Louis XVI's
most ardent defenders up to the end. He was
arrested during the Terror together with his sister
and his daughter. All three were brought up before
the Revolutionary Tribunal on the 13th of July,
1794. This was the period of wholesale condemna⁄
tions, and on that day twenty⁄eight victims were
executed. Éléonore de Faudoas refused the minis⁄
trations of a priest who had taken the oath, and
leaning on her father's arm, mounted the steps of
the scaffold making the sign of the cross. She was
eighteen.

Alexandrine de Forbin, whom Charlotte in her
letter from the Conciergerie had again commended
to the care of Barbaroux, returned to France after

a stay of several years in Switzerland. She settled down in Marseilles. When she was nearly forty, the ex-canonness of Troarn married a Customs officer, Monsieur Millière.

Charlotte's father, Monsieur de Corday d'Armont, who had been living with his aged parents at Argentan since January, 1793, learnt of the tragedy through the newspapers. He was not unduly molested. He was cross-examined on the 20th of July, and declared that since he had lost his wife, eleven years previously, his daughter had lived with him for barely a year all told. And he repeated the contents of the letter she had written him on the morning of the 9th of July just before she set out for Paris. Oddly enough, he suffered more owing to the fact that he was the father of sons who were *émigrés*. This fact led to his imprisonment for a while in 1794, and to his being outlawed in 1798. Shortly afterwards, he died at Barcelona.

His elder son, Jacques Adrien Alexis, was at that time serving in the Spanish army, after having taken part in the insurrection in Vendée. He subsequently returned to France, and in 1803 married Marthe de Hauvel.

Monsieur de Corday's younger son, Charles François Jacques, was killed at Quiberon by the side of his uncle Glatigny in an attempt to save the Royalist flag. He was eighteen.

His second daughter, Éléonore, had always lived with him after she left the Abbaye-aux-Dames. We have already mentioned that she was a hunchback. She had the reputation of being extremely witty. She died at the age of thirty-six.

The Abbé de Corday, with whom his niece Charlotte used to stay at the presbytery of Vicques, went into exile in 1792, after having being perse-cuted as a refractory priest. He took refuge in Jersey and afterwards at Winchester Castle, where the English Government had received a large number of such clergy. After his return to France, he died as Dean of Coulibœuf in 1825. He was fond of saying that Charlotte had been " another Judith sent by God to save France."

In the eyes of the Maratists, Madame de Brette-ville was guilty of having given Charlotte hospitality for two years. As soon as the death of the " Friend of the People" was made known, the good lady's house was searched. Anxious to escape the examination, she hid herself behind the bed curtains in the room behind the Lunels' shop while the police raided her premises. Fearing further investigations, she even packed her silver in a box which the carpenter buried in the floor of his workshop.

The worst fanatics demanded the destruction of her house, but they were not listened to. Every evening, however, demonstrators filed past her windows with lighted torches, carrying the bust of Marat triumphantly before them and howling ferocious songs.

Meanwhile, Augustin Leclerc continued to look after her, although he was overcome with grief at the death of Charlotte Corday. He never got over it or ceased to applaud her deed. As soon as Madame de Bretteville was able to leave her house without arousing suspicion, he took her to Verson, where she had an estate. The good lady always remained grateful to her " confidential agent ", and when, in 1799, she died at the age of seventy-five, she left him part of her property. Her house, which the Revolution spared, was pulled down and rebuilt on an improved plan in 1852.

.   .   .   .   .

On the day before the burial of Charlotte Corday's remains in the Madeleine Cemetery, Marat was given a public funeral in Paris.

On the morning of Tuesday, July the 16th, the body, which had been embalmed, was laid in state in the ancient church of les Cordeliers. The Convention had even received a request for it to be taken round all the departments. David, the artist, who had arranged the ceremony, would have liked to show the wound. But he had to abandon the idea, as if this had been done, the leprosy which had been eating into the body of the dead man would have been revealed.

In the dim light of the church, surrounded by torches and clouds of incense, raised on a platform twelve yards long, draped with the tricolour, Marat's body lay beneath a pall. His right hand fell loosely down, the fingers holding a steel pen, as though he were again about " to write for the people's good." The blood-stained dressing-gown and the bath in which he had been killed were placed beside the funeral couch. All day long the crowd filed past, convulsed with grief, crying vengeance and throwing flowers over him.

At about five o'clock in the evening, the body was placed on a hearse drawn by twelve men and surrounded by young girls in white holding branches of cypress in their hands. Behind him all the members of the Convention marched on foot, followed by the armed divisions, the popular societies and the provincial delegations. Military bands with drums hung with crape played funeral

L

marches. The crowd sang revolutionary songs. Every five minutes a gun was fired.

It was almost midnight when the endless procession, after having passed through a good part of Paris, returned to the Jardins des Cordeliers, where Marat's tomb was situated. It consisted of a granite crypt closed by a gate, and was symbolic of his strength of will and reminiscent of the subterranean depths in which he had lived. The body, placed in a lead coffin, was taken down into the vault, followed by two urns, one containing the entrails and the other the lungs. Lastly, the collected works of the " Friend of the People " were placed in the tomb. Speeches were made until far into the night.

The Jacobins' Club and the Cordeliers' Club both wanted to have Marat's heart, which had been placed in an urn made of a single block of agate set with precious stones. The Cordeliers were successful, and on the 18th of July, the urn was solemnly suspended from the ceiling of their meeting hall. Impassioned speeches rose up to it. Citizen Jullien extolled " that sacred heart, that divine organ ", and placed it above the Sacred Heart of Jesus. " O heart of Jesus, O heart of Marat ! . . . Their Jesus was only a false prophet and Marat is a god ! "

On the 19th of August, the " women of the Revolution " in their turn celebrated Marat's

memory. They marched in procession with the bust
of the divine Marat at their head, to the Place du
Carrousel, where a hollow pyramid had been erected.
Inside it had been placed Marat's bath, together
with his lamp, his desk, and his pen and paper.

A wild ferocious cult of Marat was inaugurated.
A poor couple, named Loison, who had a marionette
show in the Champs Elysées, dressed up a figure
as Charlotte Corday and made it cry " Down with
Marat ! " They were arrested and told they deserved
to be guillotined. Marat's features were reproduced
in endless variety. His bust was set up in all the
public halls, and his portrait was distributed among
the school children. Rings, tie pins and tobacco
pouches with his head on them were sold. They were
so many fetiches and proofs of patriotism. His death
inspired plays and dirges by the score. In the
schools the children were taught to make the sign
of the cross to Marat's name and to learn his *Credo*.

Children were given the name of Marat. Joachim
Murat, who afterwards became King of Naples,
asked permission from the Convention to be allowed
to change his name to Marat. In Paris, the names
of the squares and streets were altered. Anything
with the name of Montmartre was called Mont-
marat; the Rue des Cordeliers became the Rue
Marat; the Place de l'Observance the Place l'Ami

du Peuple. Throughout the provinces cenotaphs to his memory were placed beneath the Trees of Liberty, and over forty places were called after him. Le Havre de Grâce, for instance, became Havre Marat, and Neuville-sur-Saône Marat-sur-Saône.

Lastly, on the 21st of September, 1794, his supreme apotheosis was celebrated. His ashes were taken to the Panthéon in a triumphal car, followed by the Convention, the pupils of the military school, war orphans and mounted troops. Choirs sang hymns by Méhul and Cherubini in honour of the martyrs of Liberty. And while from a lower door the "unclean remains" of Mirabeau were taken away an usher solemnly read from the threshold of the Temple dedicated to great men, a decree conferring "the palm of immortality" upon Jean Paul Marat.

Five months later, on the 27th of February, 1795, in the presence of a police officer and his recorder, Marat's coffin was taken from the Panthéon and buried a short distance away in the cemetery of Sainte Geneviève !

The people had chosen another god ! The Convention, which had allowed itself to be carried along by the crowd in its mad rush for Marat, had also followed the ebb of the popular tide. The Assembly had just decreed that the honours of the Panthéon were to be awarded to citizens only ten years after their death.

Signs of the decline in Marat's popularity were not lacking. In January, the abolition of the pyramid in the Carrousel was officially decided upon, and passers-by helped the workmen in the task of demolition as they had done after the fall of the Bastille. The street-hawkers, ever ready to follow the wind, stood on the gay pile selling pamphlets entitled " The Crimes of J. P. Marat."

At this juncture, one of the newspapers published an extract from a work by Marat, the " Plan de Constitution," in which it appeared that " the Friend of the People " had advocated a return to monarchy as the only form of government suitable for France. This was the final blow to be delivered against the tottering idol ; and it fell. Marat a royalist !

On the following day, Marat's bust disappeared from the theatres and even from the Convention. Demonstrators who tried to carry the sinister emblem through the streets were arrested. Finally, young working men from the Faubourg St. Antoine marched in procession to the Jardin du Palais Royal, where they burned Marat in effigy. Gathering up the ashes in a chamber-pot, they threw them into the gutter in the Rue Montmartre, not far from the Hôtel de la Providence. And on the spot they put up an inscription, " Here is your Panthéon, Marat ! "

. . . . .

Charlotte Corday's memory underwent no such vicissitudes and changes of opinion. In many a heart she inspired a veneration no less ardent but more balanced and lasting.

Even in the crowd that surged about her on the way to the scaffold, admiration was probably almost as widespread as hatred. This is proved by the fact that while there were some who wanted to tear her to pieces there and then, others meditated rescuing her before she reached the scaffold. Conspiracies with both objects in view actually existed, and Pache, the Mayor of Paris, was warned about them, with the result that Hanriot, whom he had entrusted with the task of maintaining order, requisitioned the services of large bodies of special police.

Among the spectators, there was one man who was so dazzled by the sight of Charlotte that in a transport of mad adoration he determined to follow her to the grave. He was standing in the Rue St. Honoré, not far from the window from which Danton, Robespierre and Camille Desmoulins were watching Charlotte pass by in the cart which before very long was to convey them also to their doom. His name was Adam Lux.

At the end of the previous year, the people of Maintz, who had been converted to the ideas of the Revolution, had expressed a desire to be united to France. And Adam Lux, a deputy in the local Assembly, had been entrusted with the task of conveying this request to the Convention, who acceded to it on the 30th of March, 1793.

Adam Lux became a French citizen. He was only just twenty-eight, a fair-haired, blue-eyed sensitive dreamer. He was a doctor of medicine, married, and the father of two little girls. He proclaimed himself " a disciple of Rousseau."

He arrived in Paris full of admiration for the great principles of the Revolution, and expecting to find the Golden Age already established in France. But when he saw the reality, with its altercations, hatred, oppression and violence, he was bitterly disillusioned. The proscription of the Girondists, whose ideas he shared, was the last straw.

Overcome with disgust, he contemplated suicide, and prepared the speech he intended to deliver at the bar of the Convention before taking his leave. " I have sworn to be free or to die. Therefore it is time to die. Ever since the 2nd of June I have had a horror of life." He also expressed the hope that his death would " be more useful to the cause of Liberty than his life had been, that it would give food for reflection to the representatives of the people and mark the end of the era of violence."

He was just drawing up a sort of political testament, entitled " Avis aux Français," in which he confessed that his faith had been destroyed, when he heard of Marat's death. He read an account of Charlotte's trial, and finding that her answers expressed his own sentiments, he hurried to the route along which she was to pass to her death. When he saw her, his enthusiasm knew no bounds and he followed her to the scaffold. Thenceforward he searched for a way of escape from life. He would proclaim his admiration from the house-tops and publicly defend Charlotte. Thus he would meet his end in the noblest and most useful way. He would die for her.

It took him two days to write a eulogy of Charlotte Corday illumined and animated by passionate ardour. He sums up the drama with consummate lucidity: " A refined girl of good family, beautiful and well-educated, animated by an ardent love of her country which was in danger, she felt herself called upon to offer herself as a sacrifice for its salvation by taking the life of a man whom she held responsible for the misfortunes of the people. She reached this decision on the 2nd of June, clinched it on the 7th of July, and left her peaceful home. She confided in no one. In spite of the great heat, she took a long journey with this object in view. She arrived, without help, without advice, without anyone to comfort her. She conceived and executed a plan which she hoped would save the lives of thousands of men. She knew the fate that awaited her ! Throughout she maintained her firmness of purpose, her presence of mind and her gentle sweetness, for four whole days, until she breathed her last ! "

As he describes his impressions, his style becomes more animated : " What was my astonishment when, in addition to a courage I had expected, I beheld that imperturbable sweetness in the midst of the ferocious howling of the mob ! Her sweet and penetrating gaze ! The bright limpid light that shone in her beautiful eyes ! Her look was the look of an angel, and it reached the innermost recesses of my heart, filling it with violent emotions such as I had never before experienced ! For two hours, from the time she set out until she reached the scaffold, she maintained the same composure, the same ineffable sweetness. On the cart, with neither support nor comforter, she was exposed to the continual roar of a mob unworthy of the name of

men. She mounted the scaffold ! She died ! Charlotte, thou celestial soul, art thou really mortal ? "

Lastly, he threw down the gauntlet to the Montagne, expressing himself in terms that gave full
expression to his disillusionment: " Usurpers of the
31st of May, you who in order to escape the condign
punishment for your crimes, have deceived the
people of Paris and of all France ! I came hither to
seek the sweet reign of Liberty; I found oppression
of the just and the triumph of ignorance and crime.
I am tired of living in the midst of all the horrors
of which you are guilty and of all the misfortunes
you are preparing for my country ! Only two
hopes remain to me—either, through your kind
attentions, to die as a victim of Liberty on this
honourable scaffold, or to conspire to put an end to
your lies which are the real cause of the civil war."

Having thus provoked the Jacobins, he invited
them to allow him to die as Charlotte died. " If
they will do me the honour of sending me to the
guillotine, which I henceforward regard merely as
the altar upon which the victim is sacrificed, and
which, through the blood spilt on the 17th of July,
has lost all its shame, if, I say, they will do this, I
implore my executioners to give my severed head
the same number of blows as were given to Charlotte."

He ended these pages overflowing with a mad and tender-hearted courage, by expressing a wish " that on the very spot where she met her immortal death a statue of Charlotte Corday should be set up with the following inscription: SHE WAS GREATER THAN BRUTUS."

He was signing his own death warrant. On the 19th he published his manifesto, and three days later he was shut up in the La Force prison. There he awaited his trial for a long time. Twice he demanded that it should be held. He was condemned on the 4th of November, after a cursory examination by Fouquier-Tinville. He met his end with all the calm fortitude of his idol. " I die for Charlotte ! " he cried, as he threw himself beneath the knife, giving utterance to the thought that had upheld him from the beginning.

.   .   .   .   .   .

There was also another man who had fallen beneath the girl's sweet and powerful spell. Though he did not lay down his life for her, at least he risked it. I refer to President Montané.

As soon as the trial was over, an acrimonious altercation took place between him and the Public Prosecutor. Fouquier-Tinville accused him of having altered the last of the three questions addressed to

the jury. Referring to the murder committed by
Charlotte, the Public Prosecutor had framed this
third question in the following words: " Was it a
premeditated crime committed with criminal and
counter-revolutionary intent ? " Montané had
altered this to, " Was it a premeditated crime of
criminal intent ? "

Fouquier-Tinville accused him of having acted
partially towards Charlotte Corday and of having
shown weakness and leniency. What would he have
said had he known that Montané had suggested to
Chauveau-Lagarde to put forward a plea of insanity ?

As a matter of fact, Fouquier-Tinville's chief
grievance was that the verdict did not charge her
with being guilty of " counter-revolutionary intentions ". He had been cheated of a weapon which
would have allowed him to re-open the trial and lay
his hand upon accomplices whose heads would have
been forfeit.

In any case, Montané had risked his own head.
For on the 30th of July, the President of the Revolutionary Tribunal was arrested by order of the
Committee of Public Safety for having " changed
the wording of the third question put to the jury "
in the trial of Charlotte Corday. Fortunately for
him he was forgotten in prison, and was saved on
the 9th Thormidor (the 27th of July, 1794) when

Robespierre fell and the nightmare of the Terror faded away. He was acquitted and set free on the 13th of September, 1794.

.   .   .   .   .

The sweet calm courage of Charlotte had made such a deep impression on the public mind, that men like Chabot could not refrain from recognizing it. At a meeting of the Convention held on the 14th of July this Capuchin turkey-cock, as Marat called him, gave a report of his activities as a member of the Committee of Public Safety.

True, in speaking of the accused, he expressed himself in sympathy with the indignation and fury which had filled the Assembly when they heard the news. But, in spite of himself, his abuse ended on a note of praise. " Exaltation in her crime is painted on every feature of her face. She is capable of even greater outrages. She is one of those monsters that from time to time Nature spews up for the curse of mankind. Endowed with wit and beauty, superb in figure and bearing, she is apparently filled with a frenzied courage capable of any under-taking."

The members of the Committee of Public Safety were forced to acknowledge her extraordinary power. Fouquier-Tinville had consulted them with regard to the advisability of publishing an account of Charlotte's examination in the newspapers as well as the two letters she wrote in prison. He received the following reply: "The Committee is of opinion that it would be useless and perhaps dangerous to give too great publicity to the letters of this extraordinary woman, who has already aroused far too much interest among the evilly disposed."

"This extraordinary woman"! Thus, while they fell beneath the influence of her sweet ascendancy, the men in power also felt how dangerous it was, and tried to combat it. Leroy, one of the members of the Revolutionary Tribunal, even dared to write that "he was sorry to see condemned criminals going to the scaffold with such firmness as Charlotte Corday, and that, if he were the Public Prosecutor, he would have prisoners bled before execution to weaken their courage."

But his ferocity was not equal to that of a petitioner named Guirault who, at the sitting of the 14th of July, demanded at the bar of the Convention that new punishments should be devised for Charlotte. "Pass a special law for the occasion!" he cried. "The most terrible punishment is not enough to avenge the Nation for so terrible a crime! Savages must be taught the value of life. Instead of cutting

them off like a piece of thread, let fear of torture
disarm their parricidal hands!"

The leaders, though they refused to go to such
lengths, tried to substitute coarse caricatures for
the pleasing portraits of Charlotte. Thus, on the
21st of July, the General Council of Paris posted a
placard which was reproduced in all the news٬
papers: "This woman, who is said to be extremely
pretty, was not pretty; she was a virago more brawny
than fresh, with a manly bearing and a boyish
figure; like almost all female philosophers and
intellectuals, she was utterly lacking in charm and
was dirty in her person. She had the head of a fury;
her features were insolent, erysipelatous and vulgar,
though she had a pink and white complexion, a
rounded figure, youth and a notable frankness.
So much for a reputation for beauty during an
examination!"

But all these efforts were destined to be futile.
As soon as the ardent cult of Marat began to cool
and the popular enthusiasm had died down, the
gentle image of Charlotte again began to take pride
of place. It was found on jewels, fans and sweetmeat
boxes. Scores of painters and draughtsmen made
use of it, and almost a hundred years after her
death the Salon of 1880 alone contained four Char٬
lotte Cordays. She figured in plays all over the

world; in the course of a hundred years she provided
the inspiration for forty dramas, almost as many as
Joan of Arc in five hundred. Even fashion paid her
tribute. Women wore Charlotte Corday bonnets
and red shawls in memory of the red smock which,
wet through by the storm, clung to " the modest
and voluptuous form of Charlotte Corday."

.   .   .   .   .

But the most touching tributes came from the
men who lauded her under menace of death.

We all know André Chénier's " Ode to Charlotte
Corday." He too had enthusiastically hailed the
dawn of the Revolution, and in his poem " Le Jeu
de Paume " had celebrated the solemn oath :

O holy, triumphant immortal day !
Whose glory made brighter the sun's golden ray.

Then, like Charlotte he had been shocked to see
the Revolution descending to bloodshed. Like her,
he had pitied Louis XVI and had wanted the people
to decide his fate. His verses " To Charlotte
Corday " are indeed worthy of their heroine, for
they bear witness as much to her courage as to her
beauty :

I cannot silent stand beside thy grave
Whose blood was sacrificed sweet France to save
And shed in bringing knaves to punishment.
If, noble girl, thy frail hand seized the knife
'Twas but to shame the gods and end a life
They lent a monster for sheer devilment.

Arrested on the 7th of March, 1794, he perished
on the scaffold just two days before the deliverance
of the 9th Thermidor.

And what magnificent and pure-minded homage
Pétion rendered her when he learnt of her death!
He was anxious to correct the mistaken opinion he
had formed about her, and at a crowded meeting
of the Assembly at Caen he exclaimed: "In
ordinary times justice alone should strike the
guilty. But in present conditions the murder of
Marat is an act of national justice. A woman has
set an example to men! May they profit by the
lesson and purge France of the scoundrels who are
oppressing her!"

Louvet, who was prosecuted after the failure of
the insurrection in Normandy consecrated pages
full of burning enthusiasm to her in his hastily
written Memoirs. He envied Barbaroux for having
received the letter she had written to him from
prison: "Either nothing of what is beautiful in the

M

French Revolution will survive, or that letter will be handed down through the ages!" And the author of Faublas exulted in the fact that Charlotte had mentioned him in her examination. In his eyes this meant immortality: "Thus I have received the prize for all my works, the compensation for my sacrifices, my sufferings, and the final tortures that are in store for me. . . . Yes, come what may, I have at least received my reward—Charlotte mentioned me, and I am certain never to die!"

Salles, another of the Girondist refugees, rendered her still more touching homage. On the defeat of their party, he and his companions, Guadet, Buzot, Pétion, Barbaroux and others, had left Caen and scattered all over France. They were hunted down like wild beasts and shunned like lepers. After indescribable difficulties and sufferings, they reached St. Emilion. A noble woman, Madame Bouquey, who paid for her devotion with her life, undertook to hide them. She concealed them first in some cellars and then in two lofts. And here, in a garret where he could not stand up or light a lamp, Salles wrote a five act tragedy in verse on Charlotte Corday!

But that was not all. Salles had as his companion Guadet, who was Madame Bouquey's brother-in-

law. The three others, Pétion, Buzot and Barbaroux,
were hidden in another house. He managed to
send them his play and asked their opinion on it.
All three replied. Buzot regretted that Salles had
not kept strictly to the truth. Pétion maintained
that the author had not made the most of the part
of Charlotte Corday, " that sublime woman ", and
above all that he had depicted Robespierre and
Danton in far too flattering colours. Barbaroux
criticized the fictitious love element and patiently
line by line pointed out the weaknesses of the piece.
These three letters, all of them written at great
length, bear witness to the staggering freedom of
mind displayed by these men who were face to face
with death.

They were, in fact, denounced. On the 17th of
June, 1794, a regular army, sent out to search for
them, invaded the town. Even dogs were used to
track them down. Salles and Guadet were arrested
and guillotined at Bordeaux two days later. The
three others escaped into the woods. But on the
following day they thought the soldiers had discovered their retreat. Barbaroux tried to kill himself but the shot only broke his jaw, and he was
carried dumb and bleeding to the scaffold. A week
later the bodies of Buzot and Pétion were found in
a cornfield. They had been half eaten by the dogs

and the state of the bodies made it impossible to say how they had killed themselves.

They had merely followed in the path of death the majority of the Girondists arrested in Paris whose trial had been concluded on the previous 30th of October. Among the twenty-one who were condemned to death were Fauchet and Lauze de Perret, although the Revolutionary Tribunal had at first acquitted them of having been the accomplices of Charlotte Corday.

" She has killed us, but she has taught us how to die," observed Vergniaud, the greatest and most eloquent of them, after Charlotte's death. It was an exaggeration. The Girondists would have been lost even without her. And they would have died with fortitude without her example.

They met together for a last meal in the prison, and passed the rest of the night gravely talking together. Up to the very foot of the scaffold they sang the "Marseillaise," and the last to die was still singing after the rest had been silenced.

" They are trying to establish the Revolution by means of the Terror," said Vergniaud, this time with more justification. " I should have preferred to establish it by love."

And in fact the country was now in the strangle-hold of the Terror. If Charlotte Corday's crime

AFTERWARDS . . .

was not the cause, it at least marked the beginning
of it. She had set out to attain her end. She had
aimed at putting a stop to bloodshed. But never
before had there been such slaughter. The guillo⸗
tine worked ten times as hard as it had done before.
Such was the great lesson of the drama of which
Charlotte Corday would have felt the implacable
irony. She had proved the futility of violence !

Fate, it seems, was determined to show that even
for the sake of the highest ideal, the passion for
Peace, it is impossible to infringe with impunity,
the supreme law which enjoins respect for life.

NOTES

[1] (p. 13.)

What was the name by which Marie Anne Charlotte de Corday was usually known? According to most historians, she was called Marie in her circle.

Many of her letters, they say, were signed Marie de Corday or Marie Corday, more particularly the last which she was writing to Gustave Doulcet when the executioner entered her cell. Doulcet himself, who knew the girl well, calls her Marie Corday in his letter to Montané and in the note to the newspapers in which he protests against the accusation she made against him. Lastly, her first biographer, the German Klause, who was her contemporary, also calls her Marie Corday.

But contrary evidence can also be produced from similar sources. Laurent Esnault, a cultured bourgeois of Caen, who wrote his Memoirs during the Revolution, speaks of "the famous Charlotte Corday". Bougon-Longrais, writing to his mother a few minutes before his execution, thus apostrophises the girl: "Charlotte Corday! Oh my noble and generous friend!"

But there is even better evidence. Charles Vatel, a Versailles lawyer, who died in that town in 1885, devoted much of his life to the study of

Charlotte Corday. He left a valuable book about her, " Charlotte Corday and the Girondists ", and intended to write a general biography of his heroine. But death prevented him. However, he left to the Bibliothèque Municipale at Versailles innumerable documents which he had collected for this great work. They constitute an inexhaustible mine of information. At first one feels lost among them, and I fancy but few people have ever examined them.

Above all, Charles Vatel between 1845 and 1870 patiently collected any information that could be given by old people—servants or playfellows who had known Charlotte Corday in Normandy. When he first began his investigations, such witnesses were still numerous. They were all unanimous. They all spoke of her as " Mademoiselle Charlotte ".

Charles Vatel had collected all this evidence through his correspondents in Normandy. One of them adds to his letter the following comment which settles the matter—in the 18th century people always signed their first name even if they were not usually called by it.

Thus the girl might very well have been called Charlotte and signed herself Marie.

I vote for Charlotte.

[2] (p. 13.)

The charters of 1077 contain evidence of the existence in Normandy of a certain Robert de Corday, who served under Robert Guiscard. The Corday family took their name from the Corday estate situated in the commune of Boucé near Argentan. There is also a village called Cordey still in existence about four miles south of Falaise. The Corday crest Azure, three chevrons fracted or surmounted by a count's coronet with the motto *corde et ore*.

[3] (p. 15.)

The names of the communes in which these houses were situated have changed very little during the last hundred and forty years.

Le Ronceray, the house in which Charlotte Corday was born, is still to be seen in the commune of Champeaux.

Monsieur de Corday's manor house, afterwards known as the Ferme des Bois, is in the commune of le Renouard.

The Château de Mesnil-Imbert, belonging to Charlotte's grandfather, Corday de Cauvigny, is also in the commune of le Renouard.

The Château de Glatigny is in the commune of St. Gervais-des-Sablons.

The village of Vicques, of which the Abbé de Corday was for a long time incumbent, is situated between Jort and Morteaux-Couliboeuf.

I would remind the reader that all these houses were situated in the triangle Argentan-Falaise-Vimoutiers.

[4] (p. 16.)

She was the great-grand-daughter of Corneille and not, as has often been asserted, his great-grand-niece.

The following is a brief pedigree.

Marie, the eldest daughter of the "great Corneille" married, as her second husband, Jacques de Farcy. They had two daughters, one of whom, Françoise de Farcy, married Adrien de Corday. They had an only son, Jacques Adrien de Corday, who married Marie de Belleau de la Motte. This couple had eight children of whom one, Jacques François de Corday d'Armont married Jacqueline Charlotte Marie de Gautier des Authieux. One of their three daughters was Marie Anne Charlotte Corday.

[5] (p. 23.)

In 1788, Charlotte Corday apparently gave the Abbess, Madame de Pontécoulant, a coloured drawing on her saint's day—St. Aimée. It represented a large heart bound to smaller ones by garlands of roses held by winged angels. It was signed *CORDE*.

After Charlotte's death, Madame de Pontécoulant gave this drawing in its gilt frame to a gentleman named René. She blamed her old pupil for what she had done, declaring that no one had a right to take away a life that God had given, however great the crimes committed. She felt that a tragic fate lay in store for this girl who under her calm exterior hid so much sensitiveness and exaltation, repeating that it required a skilful and firm hand to hold her and check and guide her. She was sorry that after 1791 she saw her only at rare intervals.

No drawing by Charlotte Corday has come down to us. But several of her little poems are still in existence. The Vatel papers contain some of them; a quatrain " Le Printemps ", a sonnet " L'Arc en Ciel ", a " song without love " entitled " Le petit Mot pour Rire ", a letter in verse to her brother playfully inviting him to enter the convent. But there is nothing to prove that these various produc, tions are authentic.

As regards the subjects that Charlotte wished to master, let us point out once more that she wanted to learn Italian and English. Her friend, Mademoi, selle Levaillant, began to teach her. But the Levaillants left Caen for Rouen, and the lessons were discontinued.

[6] (p. 24.)

Many biographies of Charlotte Corday contain the letter signed Corday d'Armont, addressed to Alain, a shopkeeper in the Rue Dauphine, on the 30th of September, 1789. It deals with various orders from the Abbess and a letter of exchange made out to the said Alain, but is of no interest beyond proving her practical common sense.

Quite recently, in 1928, in an appendix to a work

entitled " Épisodes de la Révolution à Caen ", which contains the memoirs of the lawyer Laurent Esnault, Monsieur Lesage published a letter addressed to Mademoiselle Corday, c/o Madame Bretteville, opposite the church of St. Jean. This letter, which was kept back by the Black Cabinet on the 1st of June, 1793, is from a tradesman named Beausoleil of Maestricht, and proves that even after she had left the convent the girl still carried on the same business. For Beausoleil refers to one of her parcels of lace which at that time she was using as a means of barter, bemoans the increasing dearness of living, and apologises for not being able to send her linen as he could not accept *assignats* in payment.

We know of only two of the letters written by Charlotte Corday during her life at the Abbaye-aux-Dames, the letter to Alain and one written in 1788 to her cousin Madame Duhauvelle " at her estate in Authieux par Lisieux ". This lady had a little girl named Aglaé. At her request, Charlotte looked up the " Lives of the Saints " and found the life of St. Aglaé, the child's patron saint. The signature of this letter was heavily blotted out, for at the time of Marat's death it constituted an extremely compromising document. For similar reasons whole letters from her were probably destroyed, and this explains the disappearance of a large number of them.

In addition to these two letters, there is in existence one other relic of Charlotte's life at the

Abbaye-aux-Dames. All her biographers mention a little book, with emblematical illustrations, a "Typus Mundi", or "Portrait of the World", bound in white vellum with gold embellishments, which may be seen in a glass case in the Salle Révolutionnaire of the Musée Carnavalet. At the back of the half-title is written "Bought for 4 livres. Corday d'Armont, Sainte Trinité de Caen, 20th of December, 1790".

[7] (p. 25.)

Most of the biographies of Charlotte Corday state that Madame de Belzunce died a year after the murder of the young Henri de Belzunce, that is to say in 1790. But, as a matter of fact, she died in 1787. I have before me the certificate of her burial which was very kindly placed at my disposal at Caen: "In the year one thousand seven hundred and eighty-seven, on the third day of February, the body of the very reverend lady Cécile Geneviève Émilie de Belzunce de Castelmoron, born in Paris in the parish of St. Eustache, Abbess of the royal Abbey of the Holy Trinity at Caen, aged sixty-eight years, who died, fortified by the Sacraments of the Church, on the 30th of January last, was buried in the chapel of St. Benoît, situated beneath the sanctuary of the church of the said Abbey."

Vatel pointed out this repeated mistake. It is extremely important. As a matter of fact, when the young Henri de Belzunce joined the garrison at

Caen, in April, 1789, the Abbess had been dead
for two years. Moreover, she was only a distant
relative, being descended from the Castelmoron
branch of the family, while he belonged to the
Macaïe branch. Thus he had no reason for going
to the Abbaye-aux-Dames in 1789, and probably
never met Charlotte Corday there. And yet a
number of historians and novelists have made
Charlotte the mystic and inconsolable bride-elect
of the young Vicomte de Belzunce.

[8] (p. 27.)

La Fayette had fought in the American War of
Independence (1776-1782). In drawing up the plan
of the Declaration, he was inspired by The Declaration of the Rights of Man, published by the young
Transatlantic Republic, which he knew by heart,
and which was obviously based directly upon the
ideas of Montesquieu and the Encyclopædists.

Thus, as not infrequently happened in French
history, the ideas of French philosophers triumphed
in their own country only after having returned
from America.

[9] (p. 38.)

After 1840 the biographers of Charlotte Corday
call Madame de Bretteville's house Le Grand
Manoir. This is quite wrong.

Monsieur Demiau de Crouzilhac, who devoted a
treatise to the house in Caen inhabited by Charlotte

Corday, expressly says, in an article in the " Revue de Rouen " (June, 1847): " It is Lamartine who, in his History of the Girondists, muddled everything and completely misled his readers."

As a matter of fact, every block of houses in Caen used to contain and still does contain regular series of interior courtyards. Thus, according to the plan I have before me, on first entering number 148 Rue St. Jean, the real courtyard of Madame de Bretteville's house is reached, then the little court⁄ yard separating it from the house of the brewer Lacouture, and lastly, still further on, the courtyard of the Grand Manoir. Doubtless the proximity of these two houses gave rise to this curious mistake.

¹⁰ (p.41.)

I owe the description of Augustin Leclerc entirely to the documents left by Vatel to the Library of Versailles.

Contemporaries of Charlotte Corday, like Louvet and Meillan, when in their Memoirs they refer to her visits to the Intendance, always describe her as being accompanied by a servant. Later on, Chéron de Villiers mentions the name of Augustin Leclerc, but calls him " an old man⁄servant". But since he was born on the 10th of December, 1767, he was only twenty⁄six at the time !

Vatel entered into correspondence with Augustin Leclerc's daughter. Impressed by the lucidity of her remarks, he went to see her in Rouen, where she

had gone to live when she married. This was about
1860, and she must have been sixty. She had
remained touchingly devoted to her father and
extremely loyal to his memory. The precious
information this lady was able to give him confirmed
and complemented all he had been able to gather
about Augustin Leclerc in the Caen district.

[11] (p. 43.)

It was in this capacity that in April, 1792, after the
disturbances at Verson, Bougon-Longrais signed an
order from the Departmental Directorate which
bears striking testimony to his breadth of mind
and generosity of spirit. It contains, for instance,
the following passage: " Regarding it as desirable
for a true philosophic spirit and the real principles
of the Constitution to make such progress that the
most complete tolerance should cast a protecting
and soothing veil over conflicting religious opinions
as well as over the various cults which spring from
them. . . . " And further on : " It is expressly
forbidden, in the name of the Law, the Country
and Honesty, for any citizen to insult, maltreat,
pillage or commit any other outrage against any
person, whether because of differences of political
or religious opinion, on pain of being prosecuted
on a charge of violating the rights of man and of
citizenship. . . . "

In 1792, Bougon-Longrais published a book
entitled " Réflections sur la Guerre ", which made

a considerable stir and the success of which was partly responsible for his appointment to the post of Deputy Attorney-General.

His passport dated the 13th of June, 1793, may be of some interest:

Passport given to Citizen Hippolyte Bougon-Longrais, Deputy Attorney-General of the Department of Calvados, born and domiciled in Caen, aged 27 years.

Height, five foot three inches.

Hair, fair.

Eyes, blue.

Nose, long and aquiline.

Chin, round.

Face, oval.

To go into the interior of the Republic.

[12] (p. 47.)

On the 5th of November, the Municipality, followed by the National Guard, had conveyed the red flag to the scene of the disturbances, but found it unnecessary to unfurl it.

The red flag was at this time the symbol of order. Laurent Esnault, the Caen lawyer, gives the following account of it in his Memoirs: " The National Assembly had issued instructions regarding the use of the red flag at times of popular insurrection. The municipality of the place, accompanied by armed forces, was to go to the spot where the riot was in progress, carrying the red flag in a sheath; after three proclamations, if the rioters did not disperse, the red flag was to be unfurled and the order to fire given."

Everything changes !

13 (p. 47.)

Mademoiselle Levaillant, afterwards Madame Loyer de Maromme, left some Recollections of Charlotte Corday, which she confided to the care of a young relative, Casimir Périer, father of the man who was for a short time President of the Republic. He published them in 1862 with a guar‹ antee of their authenticity.

Unfortunately, these memoirs are full of mis‹ takes. Thus she says: "Madame de Belzunce did not long survive her nephew." But she died two years before the Vicomte de Belzunce. And speak‹ ing of Charlotte's father, she says: "The old noble‹ man was royalist to the backbone." But various writings left by Monsieur de Corday d'Armont, that is to say his "Mémoires aux Assemblées Provinciales", his two "Mémoires sur le droit d'Ainesse" and his "Principes de Gouvernement" are sufficient proof that he was a Liberal.

Her description of Charlotte's arrival at Madame de Bretteville's is obviously pure fabrication. Accord‹ ing to her, the old lady did not know this relative "who had descended upon her from the clouds". Now, Augustin Leclerc tells us that Madame de

Bretteville had paid the expenses of Charlotte's last years as a boarder at the convent and that during her stay there she had received her both at Caen and Verson.

I did not think it necessary to give the oft-repeated story of the dinner at Madame de Bretteville's. But here again truth and falsehood are mixed. Madame de Maromme says that the dinner took place on St. Michael's Day, 1891, that is to say on the 29th of September. And she declares that it was during this dinner that Bishop Fauchet's solemn entry in procession took place beneath the windows of the house. But this solemn entry took place on the 11th of May. And, according to Laurent Esnault's Memoirs, Fauchet left for Paris on September the 28th.

At this dinner, Madame de Bretteville and Charlotte had the pleasure of Madame Levaillant's company, as well as that of Monsieur de Corday d'Armont, his daughter Eléonore and his young son, and Monsieur Tournélis, a second cousin of the hostess. The two young men were on their way to Coblenz. The King's health was proposed. Everybody got up except Charlotte, who remained seated, leaving her glass on the table. There was an uncomfortable pause. Shortly afterwards, Fauchet, the constitutional Bishop, passed beneath the windows surrounded by a rowdy crowd of people shouting " *Vive la Nation !* " The two young men wished to shout " *Vive le Roi !* " Charlotte told Monsieur de Tournélis to be quiet, but he hotly defended himself. Had she not just given expression to her own sentiments ? To which, with her usual logic, she replied that in refusing to drink the King's health she was harming only herself, while if he cheered the King he ran an utterly futile risk of endangering the lives of everybody present.

Although Madame de Maromme's Memoirs are sometimes inaccurate in detail, on the whole they bear the imprint of truth. One feels, for instance, that the following picture of Charlotte Corday is true to life: " Her skin was dazzlingly white and extraordinarily fresh. She had a complexion like milk and roses with the velvety surface of the peach. The texture of her skin was so fine that one imagined one was looking at the blood circulating under the petal of a lily. She blushed extremely easily and then became really ravishingly lovely. Her faintly clouded eyes were large and well shaped and extremely beautiful; her chin, somewhat prominent, did not mar a whole which was charming and full of distinction. The expression on her beautiful face was inexpressibly sweet, as was also the sound of her voice, which fell with unsurpassed harmony and enchantment on the ear. Never have I seen any٭ thing purer and more angelic than her expression or more attractive than her smile. Her light chest٭ nut hair suited her face admirably; in short, she was a superb woman."

When Mademoiselle Levaillant left Caen for Rouen, Charlotte Corday wrote her about a dozen letters. Her mother wanted to burn them so as to be on the safe side after Marat's death. But two escaped destruction, and Casimir Périer published them at the end of Madame Maromme's Memoirs. They are interesting chiefly on account of their naturalness. Charlotte herself speaks in them.

I give the principal passages in the first letter:

"March 1792

" Can it really be possible, my dear friends, that while I was accusing you of laziness you had fallen a victim to that terrible small-pox? You must indeed be glad to have got over it and thankful that it has spared your face—a favour it does not always deign to accord pretty people!

"You were ill and it was impossible for me to know it! Promise me, my darling, that if you get such a foolish idea into your head again you will tell me beforehand, as I think nothing is more cruel than not to know what is happening to one's friends.

"You ask me for news. At the present moment, dear heart, nothing is happening in our town. All the sensible people have girded up their loins and fled. Your curses on the place have been fulfilled, and if the grass is not growing in the streets, it is only because it is not the season for it. The Faudoas have gone and even part of their furniture. Monsieur de Cussy has charge of the flags; he is rather sweet on Mademoiselle Fleuriot. With this general exodus, we are extremely quiet and the fewer the people the less likelihood there is of insurrection. . . .

"If I had only myself to consider, I should increase the number of refugees in Rouen, not because I am frightened, but so as to be with you, dear heart, and have the advantage of taking lessons from you. I should not hesitate to choose you as my foreign

" That's enough about them ! All the people you mention are in Paris. To-day the rest of our good folk leave for Rouen, and we shall be almost alone. What can one expect ? Nobody is bound to do the impossible. I should have been altogether delighted to settle down in your district, especially as we are threatened with insurrection in the near future. But one can die only once and my consolation in the midst of all these horrors is that I should be no loss to anybody unless my love for you means anything to you. Perhaps you would be surprised, my darling, if you could see how full of fears I am; but if you were here you would share them, I am sure. I could tell you nice tales about the state of our town and the excitement everywhere !

" Good-bye, my angel. I must stop, because I can't write any more with this pen, and I am afraid I have already delayed sending off this letter too long—the carriers are due to go to-day. I beg you to act as my go-between and give Madame Levaillant my kindest regards and best wishes. My aunt asks me to tell her, and you too, that she will always remember the happy days she had with you, and hopes you will never cease to count on her devotion. I will not say anything about my love for you. I want you to take that for granted, without my having to repeat the same thing over and over again."

14 (p. 86.)

Marat's journal was first called " L'Ami du Peuple ", then, after the 26th of September, 1792, " Le Journal de la République ", and lastly, after the 14th of March, 1793, " Le Publiciste de la République Française ".

In the last number of the " Publiciste de la République ", dated the 13th of July, 1793, that is to say the very day of his death, Marat recommended murder by means of the dagger! Thus he too raised the dagger of Brutus!

He reproached Carra, who had been sent to Dumouriez, for not having stabbed the King of Prussia before he left: "What were you doing?" he exclaimed. "Did the Roman consuls, whom you sometimes ape, behave like that? Where was the dagger of Brutus?"

[15] (p. 87.)

It was during his detention in the Château de Caen that Romme, the Member of the Convention, sketched out his Republican Calendar. The work was completed by Fabre d'Eglantine. Lalande also, apparently, collaborated in the task.

[16] (p. 95.)

The tone of this placard is strangely ironical. It referred with equal contempt to the Maratists and the aristocrats. The following sentence occurred in it: " The Assembly unanimously decrees that the general call to arms shall be immediately sounded; that the battalions of the National Guard shall meet in the Cours National at three o'clock in the after‹ noon, and that, since it is a question of raising a battalion to fight anarchy and the anarchists by hastening to the help of our brethren in Paris, the Aristocrats and the Maratists are excused from attending this meeting."

[17] (p. 99.)

The letter ran as follows:

" Caen,
" July 7th, 1793.
" The year II of the Republic
one and indivisible.

" I am sending you, my dear friend, a few interesting books which ought to be circulated.

" Salle's work on the Constitution is the one which at the present juncture will have the most influence. I will send you a fairly large supply of copies at the earliest opportunity.

" I am sending this letter *viâ* Rouen, and beg you to use your influence on behalf of a young lady who is one of our fellow citizens. It is merely a matter of getting some papers from the Ministry of the Interior, and sending them to me at Caen. The lady who is bringing the letter is interested in the matter, and her request seemed so justifiable that I did not hesitate to do my best to help her.

" Farewell ! I embrace you and salute your daughters, Marion and our friends. Send me news of your son.

" All goes well here and it will not be long before we are under the walls of Paris."

[18] (p. 99.)

The following is Charlotte Corday's passport. The words in italics are written in by hand.

The Country—Liberty—Equality
Department of Calvados
Caen District

Passport for Citizen *Marie Corday*, native of *Mesnil Imbert*, domiciled in *Caen*, of the munici pality of *Caen*, department of *Calvados*, age 24 *years*, height five *foot one inch*, hair and eyebrows *chestnut*, eyes *grey*, forehead *high*, nose *long*, mouth *medium size*, chin *round* and *cleft*, face *oval*.

Give her help and assistance in case of need on her way to *Argentan*.

Delivered at the common hall of Caen, on the 8th of April 1793, the year II of the French Republic by us *Fossez Senior*, municipal officer.

Drawn up by us, the undersigned registrar, and the said citizen *Corday*, signed:

MARIE CORDAY

HENI, *Registrar*.

On the back we find:

Examined at the Common Hall of Caen for the purpose of going to Paris.

The 23rd of April, 1793, the year II of the Republic.

ENGUELLARD, *Municipal Officer*.

[19] (p. 112.)

These arcades and the buildings above them had been completed in 1786. They have not changed since. The Galeries de Bois, built in 1786 and done away with in 1830, occupied the site of the present Galerie d'Orléans. No enquiry was made about the cutler who sold Charlotte Corday the knife. He is supposed to have been Sieur Badin, of 177, The Arcade.

[20] (p. 114.)

Simonne Evrard had, so to speak, taken Marat to her bosom out of admiration. She was twenty-seven and he was fifty. Though not beautiful, she was extremely smart. The flat in the Rue des Cordeliers was rented in her name. Out of gratitude Marat had promised to marry her. The following is the curious agreement by which he undertook to do so.

" As the fine qualities of Mademoiselle Simonne Evrard have won my heart, the homage of which was already hers, I leave as a pledge of my good faith during the journey I am about to take to London, this sacred undertaking to give her my hand as soon as I return. If all my tender feelings for her are not sufficient guarantee of my fidelity, may forgetfulness of this undertaking cover me with shame.

" Paris, the 1st of January, 1792,

" Jean Paul Marat,

" The Friend of the People."

Nevertheless, she was taken for his sister in their circle. Thus the *commissionnaire*, Laurent Bas, in his cross-examination and in all his declarations and descriptions of what occurred, always referred to her as " the sister ". After the tragedy she became " Marat's widow ". One of Marat's brothers and two of his sisters even wished to show their gratitude to the young woman by giving this union public recognition. And they sent to the " Journal

de la Montagne " the following declaration which
appeared on the 26th of August, 1793 :—" Although
we already knew of the great services rendered by
Citizen Evrard to Citizen Marat, her husband, we
thought it necessary, in order to give her action
all the publicity demanded by our gratitude, to call
to witness those persons who knew the straits to
which our brother had been reduced by the sacrifices
he had made in aiding and abetting the Revolution.

" Full of admiration and gratitude, we hereby
declare that it is to the care of our good and beloved
sister that the family of her husband owes the last
years of his life.

" We therefore declare that we have the greatest
satisfaction in fulfilling the wishes of our brother
by recognizing Citizen Evrard as our sister."

[21] (p. 117.)

The tale goes that before she returned to Marat's
house, Charlotte had her hair dressed and lightly
powdered at the Hôtel de la Providence by the
hairdresser Férieux. He is even supposed to have
seen the knife lying on the mantelpiece. I did not
give this anecdote in the body of my book as it
appeared to me of doubtful authenticity. In the
first place, a great many people mistakenly imagined
they had seen Charlotte in Paris—the official
Hénoque and the Lebourgeois woman, for instance.
Most important of all, the proprietress and the
waiter at the hotel described Charlotte's most trivial

movements and actions, the visitors she received etc., giving a detailed account of what Lauze de Perret looked like and how he was dressed. They said nothing about Férieux.

[22] (p. 118.)

When she was examined, first at the judicial enquiry and then at her trial, Charlotte persisted in saying that she went twice altogether to Marat's house, once in the morning and once in the evening.

But many historians are inclined to believe that she went three times, twice in the morning and once in the evening.

I myself am of opinion that Charlotte spoke the truth; she never lied except when she was forced to do so. So she went to the Rue des Cordeliers only twice.

Then why should so many writers maintain that she went three times? The third visit, I think, was an invention on the part of the porter's wife, Madame Pain, who was anxious to cover herself and disclaim all responsibility. She invented a first visit when she categorically refused to give the girl access even to the house, and maintained that the latter forced her way in at her second attempt without being seen.

If we examine the evidence given at the judicial enquiry, we find that Madame Pain and the cook Jeannette Maréchal were gossiping in the lodge when Charlotte first presented herself. The porter's wife absent-mindedly pointed out Marat's flat. The two women were still gossiping when Charlotte came down. All this Jeannette Maréchal ingenu- ously confessed in the wording of her evidence before Judge Foucaut.

The two chatterboxes must have allowed the girl to go up on the one and only occasion that she presented herself in the morning. It was later in the day that Madame Pain invented another earlier visit, at which Charlotte failed to gain admittance, and this visit, of which there is no proof, was thrust down the throats of all concerned by Madame Pain herself.

23 (p. 125.)

On leaving Marat's house, was Charlotte Corday taken to the Committee of Public Safety to undergo another examination before being shut up in the Abbaye Prison? Opinions are divided on the matter.

I always thought that no further examination took place. Firstly, there is no evidence of it, although the minutest details of the trial have come down to us. Secondly, Charlotte does not mention it in her letter to Barbaroux.

I think the following provides convincing proof. Drouet, as the representative of the Committee of Public Safety, went to Marat's house, and conducted Charlotte Corday to the Abbaye Prison. On the 14th of July, in the Convention, he gave an account of what he had done. He went up on to the rostrum directly after Chabot, who had just related what he had seen at Marat's house. Drouet began as follows: " I will say nothing of what took place at Marat's. I took the murderess to the Abbaye. . . . " He described the fury of the mob and what he said to calm it. There was never any question of a halt and a fresh examination. Clearly the cab went direct from the Rue des Cordeliers (the present Rue de l'École de Médecine) to St. Germain-des-Prés. It did not take the roundabout way past the Tuileries, where the Committee of Public Safety held its sessions.

[24] (p. 127.)

The report of the search made at the Hôtel de la Providence runs as follows:

" We found in the said chest-of-drawers a striped *bazin* wrapper, unmarked; a pink silk petticoat and a white cotton petticoat, both unmarked; two chemises, marked C.D.; two pairs of cotton stockings, one white and one grey, unmarked; a little sleeveless white linen dressing-gown marked with two Cs back to back; four white handkerchiefs, one of which was marked C.D.; two lawn caps; two lawn fichus; one green gauze fichu; a silk fichu with a red band; a parcel of ribbons of various colours.

" Whereas the said effects were all we found in the said room, we wrapped them up in an unfolded towel, marked with the letter B., which we also found in the said room, and this parcel we sealed with our commissioner's seal in two places before sending it to the police."

On the 16th of July, a messenger from the Mairie took this parcel to the Registrar's Office at the Conciergerie. It was registered as follows:

"The girl Corday. Parcel of the 16th of July.

"Citizen Barutot, a messenger from the Mairie, came and deposited a parcel wrapped up in a towel sealed in two places, which he said belonged to Citizeness Corday, the murderess of Marat, and which the police officers told him to bring."

²⁵ (p. 127.)

This is the letter, written partly at the Abbaye and partly at the Conciergerie, which, according to Louvet, " is destined to go down through the ages." Peace is mentioned in ten places.

" From the Abbaye Prison, in the cell vacated by Brissot, on the second day of the preparations for Peace.

" You asked me, Citizen, to send you an account of my journey. I will not bore you with anecdotes. I travelled with good Montagnards whom I allowed to chatter to their hearts' content, and as their conversation was as stupid as their persons were disagreeable, I found it all the easier to go to sleep. I might almost say I woke up only on reaching Paris.

" One of my travelling companions, who doubtless likes women when they are asleep, thought I was the daughter of an old friend of his. He endowed me with a fortune I do not possess, gave me a name which I have never heard, and in the end offered me his hand and all his worldly goods. 'We are playing a regular comedy,' I said, when I began to grow tired of his attentions. 'It is unfortunate that so much talent should not have an audience. I am going to fetch our fellow-travellers so that they may share the entertainment.' And in a very bad temper he left me. During the night he murmured plaintive ditties which were extremely soporific in their effect. At last, when we reached Paris, I got rid of him, refusing to give him either my own or my father's address. He wanted to ask my father for my hand. He was very cross when he left me.

"I did not know that the gentleman who examined me had questioned my travelling companions, and to save them the trouble of entering into explanations, I said I did not know any of them. In this I followed my oracle, Raynal, who says that tyrants do not deserve to be told the truth. It was through the lady who travelled with me that they found out I knew you and that I had spoken to Duperret. You know how resolute Duperret is; he told them the exact truth in answer to their questions. I confirmed his evidence by my own. There is nothing against him, but his resolution was regarded as a crime. I confess I was very much afraid they would find out I had spoken to him. I regretted having done so when it was too late, and I tried to make up for my mistake by making him promise to join you. But he was too obstinate to make any such promise. Knowing that he and everybody else were innocent, I deter‹ mined to carry out my plan.

" Can you believe it, Fauchet is in prison for being my accom‹ plice, Fauchet who did not even know of my existence ! But they don't like having only an insignificant woman to offer to the shade of that great man ! Pardon me, ye men, the word is an insult to your kind ! He was a ravening monster, who would have devoured the whole of France through civil war. But now, *vive la paix !* Thank God, he was not a Frenchman born. Four of the members were present at my first examination. Chabot looked like a madman. Legendre insisted that he had seen me in the morning at his house. I never gave this man a thought. I do not think he is great enough to be the tyrant of this country, and I had no wish to punish so many people. All

o

those who have never set eyes on me before said they had known me for ages.

" I hear that Marat's last words have been printed. I don't know that he ever gave utterance to any; at all events I can tell you what were the last words he said to me. After writing down the names of all of you, and the names of the members of the Calvados Government who are at Évreux, he said, to console me, that in a few days he would have you all guillotined in Paris. These last words decided his fate. If the department sets up his bust opposite St. Fargeau's, it ought to have these words engraved in letters of gold.

" I shall not tell you any details about the great event. The newspapers will tell you all about that. I confess that what finally decided me was the courage with which our volunteers enlisted on the 7th of July. You remember how charmed I was, and I promised myself that I would make Pétion regret the suspicions he harboured with regard to my feelings. ' Would you be sorry if they did not go ? ' he asked me. In short, I came to the conclusion that it was foolish for so many brave men to try for the head of one man whom they might miss or who might drag down a number of worthy citizens with him. He did not deserve the honour. A woman's hand was enough ! I confess that I made use of a treacherous trick to induce him to receive me; but the end justifies the means in such circumstances.

" When I left Caen, I counted upon sacrificing him on the summit of the Mountain; but he was no longer attending the Convention. I wish I had kept your letter; then they would have been convinced that I had no accomplices. But all that will be cleared up. We are such good Republicans in Paris that nobody can believe that a futile woman, who would never have been of any use however long she lived, could possibly sacrifice herself in cold blood to save her country. I was expecting to die at any moment, but brave men who are really above all praise saved me from the excusable fury of those whom I had made miserable. As I really acted in cold blood, the crying of some women upset me. But if one saves one's country one must not think of the price that has to be paid.

"May Peace be established as quickly as I hope it will. An important step has been taken in that direction without which we should never have had it. I have been revelling in Peace for the last two days; my country's good is my own. The reward for every act of devotion is far greater than the pain one feels in deciding to perform it. I am afraid they may worry my father a little; he already has quite sufficient cause for distress in losing me. If any of my letters are found in his possession, most of them are portraits of you. If they contain any jokes at your expense, I beg you to overlook them. I gave way to the frivolity of my nature. In my last letter I led him to believe that I was terrified at the horrors of civil war, and was going to England. At that time my idea was to remain unknown, to kill Marat publicly and be killed myself at once, leaving the people of Paris to make a vain search to discover who I was.

"I beg you, Citizen, you and your colleagues, to take up the cudgels on behalf of my relatives and friends if they are molested. I say nothing to my dear aristocratic friends whose memory I keep in my heart. I have hated only one person in my life, and I have proved the strength of my hatred. But there are thousands whom I even love more than I hated him. A lively imagination and a tender heart gave promise of a stormy life, and I beg those who may possibly regret me to remember this and rejoice to see me enjoying my rest in the Elysian Fields with Brutus and the other heroes of old.

"Among moderns there are few true patriots who know how to die for their country; selfishness accounts for nearly every, thing. What a sorry people to found a Republic! But at least the foundations of Peace must be laid, and the Government will follow as best it can. At all events, the Mountain will certainly not rule France; you may take my word for that!

" I am treated with the utmost consideration in prison; the *concierges* are the best and kindest of souls. I have been given some gendarmes to prevent me from being bored; that was all right during the day, but at night it is extremely disagreeable. I complained of the indecency, but the Committee did not think fit to pay any attention. I think it was Chabot's idea; only a Capuchin could have thought of such a thing! I while away the time writing songs. I give Valady's couplet to anybody who wants it. I have assured the people of Paris that we are taking up arms only against anarchy, which is absolutely true.

" I have been transferred to the Conciergerie, and the gentlemen of the grand jury have promised to send you my letter; so I am continuing it. I have undergone a long examination; please get it if it is published. At the time of my arrest I had an Address on me which I had written to the Friends of Peace. I cannot send it to you. I shall ask for it to be published, though I expect it will be useless.

" I had an idea last night of presenting my portrait to the department of Calvados, but the Committee of Public Safety, to whom I addressed my request, have not answered, and now it is too late.

" I beg you, Citizen, to communicate my letter to Citizen Bougon, Deputy AttorneyGeneral of the department. I am not addressing it to him for various reasons. In the first place, I am not sure that he is in Évreux just now, and secondly I am afraid that as he is naturally kindhearted, he may be distressed by my death. But I think he is a good enough Citizen to find consolation in the hope of Peace. I know how much he longs for it, and I trust that in paving the way to it I have fulfilled his wishes. If any of my friends ask to see this letter, I beg you not to refuse anybody.

"I have to have a counsel for the defence; it is the rule. I chose mine from the Mountain—Gustave Doulcet. I expect he will refuse the honour. I thought of asking for Robespierre or Chabot! I shall ask to be allowed to dispose of the rest of my money, and if my request is granted, I offer it to the wives and children of the brave men of Caen who set out for the deliverance of Paris.

"It is astonishing that the people allowed me to be transferred from the Abbaye to the Conciergerie. It affords fresh proof of their moderation. Tell the good people of Caen this. They occasionally allow themselves the luxury of a little insurrection, which it is not easy to keep in hand.

"To-morrow, at eight o'clock, my trial begins. Probably by midday I shall have lived, to use a Latin expression. People must believe in the valour of the men of Calvados since even the women of the district are capable of determination. I have no idea how my last moments will be spent, and it is the end that crowns the achievement. There is no need for me to feign indifference to my fate, for up to the present I have not felt the smallest fear of death. I never had any regard for life except as a means of being useful.

"I hope that to-morrow Duperret and Fauchet will be set free. They say that the latter took me to the Convention, to one of the galleries. But why should he want to take a woman there? As a deputy he had no business in the galleries, and as a Bishop he had no business to be in the company of women. I make this little correction. But Duperret has nothing to reproach himself with. Marat will not go to the Panthéon, although he thoroughly deserved to do so. I entrust you with the task of getting together the material for his funeral oration.

"I hope you will not cease to take an interest in Madame Forbin's business. This is her address if you find it necessary to write to her: Alexandrine Forbin, Mandresie, near Zurich,

Switzerland. I beg you to tell her that I love her with all my heart.

"I am going to write a word to my father; I shall not say anything to our other friends. All I ask of them is to forget me quickly; their grief would disgrace my memory. Tell General Wimpffen that I believe I have helped him to win more than one battle by paving the way to Peace.

"Farewell, Citizen! I commend myself to the memory of the true Friends of Peace.

"The prisoners in the Conciergerie, far from insulting me like the people in the streets, looked as though they pitied me. Misfortune always arouses sympathy. This is my last reflection.

"Tuesday the 16th at eight o'clock in the evening.

"Corday."

26 (p. 129.)

In connection with her stay in this prison I have found in three places in the Vatel papers evidence of an anecdote which has been widely circulated. In a dark corridor Charlotte apparently trod on a kitten's paw making the animal howl with pain. "Oh! that upsets me much more than having killed Marat!" she exclaimed. This is such an obvious comparison that it makes the incident dubious.

27 (p. 132.)

The following is the letter, of which Gustave Doulcet knew nothing until after the execution. The caution of the Public Prosecutor should be noted.

" Paris

" This 16th of July, 1793 of the Republic.

" Citizen,

" I have the honour to inform you that Marie-Anne-Charlotte Corday, who lies under accusation of having murdered Marat, has chosen you as her counsel, notwithstanding that it was pointed out to her, both by the President and myself, that a deputy could not act as her counsel, since he was tied by the duties of his position. But as she named you it is my duty to inform you of the fact and to tell you that the case opens to-morrow at eight o'clock punctually. Furthermore, I beg to say that, foreseeing the possibility of business preventing you from accepting this invitation, I have appointed an assistant counsel.

" With fraternal greetings,

" The Public Prosecutor of the extraordinary revolutionary Tribunal

" Fouquier-Tinville."

This assistant counsel was a lawyer named Guyot. We know that he did not attend the court.

28 (p. 133.)

One of the jurymen was the magistrate Fualdés, who was murdered in 1817. This famous crime has always remained a mystery. A legend sprang up that Fualdés undertook to save Charlotte Corday or to help her to escape, but that, failing to keep his promise, he paid the penalty of his life twenty-four years later for what amounted to an act of treachery. This is a most unlikely tale.

[29] (p. 139.)

He thought that Marat had read the second letter
in which Charlotte appealed to his humanity and
which she kept on her. Marat saw only the first
letter, sent by the *petite poste* in which she proposed
to give him information regarding the Normandy
plot.

Montané was not the only one to be guilty of this
confusion. In David's picture, " The Death of
Marat ", this second letter, which Marat never saw,
is spread out on the board across the bath. " Surely
it is enough that I am unhappy for me to have
a right to your protection " can be distinctly
read.

This picture is in the Revolution Room in Versailles Museum. The mistake will be perpetuated
for centuries to come ! People will continue to
believe that Marat opened his door to Charlotte
Corday out of kindness of heart !

One of the Museum keepers to whom I made
this observation replied with some wit: " It is a
forgery perpetrated in a public painting."

[30] (p. 146.)

The portrait by Hauer is now in the Versailles
Museum. It hangs next to David's picture of Marat's
death. Underneath the picture is the following
inscription:

Marie Anne Charlotte Corday de Armans,
native of the parish
of St. Saturnin des Lignerets,
aged 25 years, beheaded in Paris
the 17th of July, 1793
for having stabbed Marat.
Done from life by Hauer.

There is also another portrait " done from life ".
This is a pastel by Brard, sketched during the
journey from the prison to the scaffold. It is in the
Mancel collection which was left to the town of
Caen. On the back of the picture is the following
inscription:

Marie Anne Charlotte Corday,
painted from life, on her way to execution
by Brard.

On a strip of paper are the following lines:

Marat apart—a monster and exception—
Homicide prepense is assination.

These are, I believe, the only two portraits done
from life. But there are innumerable others.

[31] (p. 153.)

Apparently, Charlotte Corday's skull was preserved. The novelist Esquiros saw it in 1840 at
Monsieur de St. Aubin's house. It afterwards came
into the possession of Duruy, and subsequently
into that of Roland Bonaparte. It was exhibited at

the International Exhibition of 1889. Prince Roland Bonaparte intended to furnish proofs of its authen⸝ticity, but I do not think he ever did so. It is an extremely dubious " relic ". Yet it attracted the attention of scientific men like Lombroso, Topinard and Benediks who took exhaustive measurements of it.

Among Anatole France's papers I found cuttings from newspapers of 1890 with notes in his own handwriting all relating to this skull. They include everything from the long and learned article in the " Temps " to the light fantasy in " La Vie Parisi⸝enne ". I merely mention this to show the interest which the memory of Charlotte Corday inspired even a hundred years after her death.

³² (p. 153.)

Was Charlotte Corday's chastity instrumental in producing a state of spiritual exaltation which prompted her to the crime she committed ?

Some of her contemporaries declare that it was. Harmand de la Meuse wrote as follows : " The doctors were of opinion that Charlotte Corday was physically so constituted as to produce the exaltation necessary for committing a murder. This physical cause is known as *moral purity.*"

When Ponsard had his " Charlotte Corday " produced at the Comédie Française on the 23rd of March, 1850, a dramatic critic, who signed himself Th. de B.[1] wrote, without beating about the

[1] Théodore de Banville.—*Translator*

bush: " If Corneille's grand/daughter had been a wife and mother, the fair young blood that surged through her brain and heart and made her mad with fanaticism would have filled her breasts with milk to nourish beautiful children like the child she kissed with tears in her eyes at the Palais Royal. . . . The angels who whispered into the ear of the heroine of Vaucouleurs were the same as those who urged Charlotte Corday to kill Marat; they were her youth, her life and her rebellious blood. . . . The most outrageous part of the glory and shame of these two girl martyrs was the virginity which our barbarous laws make a duty."

Nowadays many medical men, novelists and scientists are inclined to believe that chastity creates a state of morbidity and gives rise to serious moral upheavals.

My own conclusion has been slowly reached. I do not believe that chastity has any serious effect upon moral health. A cloister is no madder than a harem.

True, it would be easy to find signs of nervous disorder and obsession in Charlotte Corday—her readiness to blush, her physical insensibility, and her relief after the crime. But similar stigmata might be found in anybody. Nobody is absolutely normal. And we should beware of these *a posteriori* conclusions and this insistence on classification, in a region where all is indefinite.

Lombroso hesitated to class political and ordinary criminals together, or to apply the same methods of investigation to them. In this connection he writes in his " Criminal Man " : " We feel how cruel it must seem to compare common criminals with those who represent an excess of human kindness. . . . The very fact of trying to examine them too closely beneath the light of psychiatry makes us appear like a man trying to study the lovely curves of the Venus de Medici by means of the compass, without regard for the sublime purity of the whole.

" O saintly souls, devoted to an idea, forgive us ! We feel that your mere appearance is sufficient to raise mankind and make up for the all too large number of those for whom vulgar enjoyment is the only aim in life ! "

We must remember that from her earliest childhood Charlotte Corday had before her eyes the stern example of the heroes of old as depicted by her ancestor Corneille; we must remember that she lived at a time of herd madness, like the period of the Great War, during which contempt for life, strenuousness and violence were in the air.

These dominating influences exercised on a supersensitive soul are quite sufficient to explain the action of the woman who has been called the Angel of Assassination, the Joan of Arc of the Revolution, but whom I regard as having been first and foremost the Virgin of Peace.

THE END

INDEX

PRINTED IN GREAT BRITAIN BY PURNELL AND SONS
PAULTON (SOMERSET) AND LONDON

7045 — 1148

4 . 1   6.04 V.

3.37   502
—————

5.87   7.02 .